Welcome to Britain
[Revised Edition]

by
Tim Knight

TSURUMI SHOTEN

Welcome to Britain [Revised Edition]

Copyright © 2012 and 2018 by Tim Knight

All rights reserved.

No part of this book may be used or reproduced without the written permission of the publisher.

Photo credits

ダイソン株式会社
Tim Knight
Simon Knight
© UK Parliament/Jessica Taylor
© skvoor—Fotolia.com
© lilufoto—Fotolia.com
© Klaus-Peter Adler—Fotolia.com
© Artur Marciniec—Fotolia.com
© iStockphoto.com/Jeremy Wee

Preface

Thank you for choosing this book and welcome to Britain!

The 16 chapters in this book introduce various topics about Britain specifically for Japanese people. Since the previous edition, a new chapter has been added to address the topic of Britain's decision to leave the European Union, following a referendum. This has created an air of uncertainty and instability, but how things develop will surely be interesting to watch. Other parts of the book have been updated to take into account various changes in the last few years.

The format of the book remains the same. The readings in each chapter are divided into three parts. This makes the readings more manageable and less daunting for students who may be put off by having to read long texts without a break. Two reading comprehension questions follow both parts 1 and 3, with one question asked about the shorter middle section.

Breaking the readings into three parts also makes the material more flexible for the teacher because it is possible to do other sections before parts 2 or 3 to vary the style or pace of the lesson. The five Structure Practice questions, which follow the readings, challenge students' knowledge of English vocabulary and grammar. Then five Listening Challenge questions require students to be active by both listening, and writing.

One key point about the structure practice and listening challenge questions is that they contain further information about that chapter's topic. They are not merely repeated facts from the readings. This means that while tackling these tasks to challenge their vocabulary, grammar, comprehension and listening skills, students can learn more interesting things about the topic.

The last, but equally important, section in each chapter is Going Further. Here are questions for readers to consider, for discussion and/or further research. These questions give students a chance to reflect on their new knowledge of British society, to share their opinions, sometimes in comparison with what they know of Japan, or perhaps as prompts to find out more about the topic.

I hope you enjoy engaging with the information and ideas in this book about Britain. I also hope you enjoy the photographs which are meant to be visually appealing and complementary to the text.

Tim Knight

Table of CONTENTS

Chapter 1   The United Kingdom? *1*

Chapter 2   Multicultural Britain *7*

Chapter 3   The UK and the EU *13*

Chapter 4   Tea *19*

Chapter 5   Social class *25*

Chapter 6   Schools and education *31*

Chapter 7   University students and higher education *37*

Chapter 8   Women in society *43*

Chapter 9   Science, inventions and business *49*

Chapter 10   Politics and government *55*

Chapter 11   Food *61*

Chapter 12   Music and fashion *67*

Chapter 13   Fantasy and castles *73*

Chapter 14   Language *79*

Chapter 15   The arts *85*

Chapter 16   Homes, gardens and the countryside *91*

Chapter 1

The United Kingdom?

Vocabulary Focus

Match the words in the table with their definition below. Write the word on the line.

accommodate	dis- (prefix)
complicated	invention
contribute	nationality

contribute   1. do something to help

_____   2. not (at the front of a word)

_____   3. to please or satisfy someone, provide living space

_____   4. difficult to understand or do things with

_____   5. related to the country where you were born, or where you have a right to be a citizen

_____   6. a new idea or newly made

Part 1   Background

Let's begin with a question: if someone asks you what nationality you are, what would you say? Would it be easy to answer? Probably, yes. But if you ask someone from the UK what nationality they are, the answer you get could be *British*, or *English*, or *Scottish*, or *Welsh*, or *Irish*, or a combination like British *and* Welsh. It largely depends on their point of view, but some people will give their answer quickly and easily; some will pause and think first; and some will give an answer that you may not understand well[1].

This chapter will try to establish why this is so. First, there are four countries called, in order of size: England, Scotland, Wales and Northern Ireland. The UK's full name is the United Kingdom of Great Britain and Northern Ireland. People often call the group of countries *Britain*. This book often will too. What you shouldn't do is say 'England' if you want to include the three smaller countries. Even the terms *Igirisu* or *Eikoku* are disliked by some people, especially from Scotland and Wales, because they seem to suggest England is the same as Britain. England dominates the others with its bigger size and population, but the history of the UK is short compared with the history of the countries separately.

Strictly, Great Britain is the land consisting of the countries England, Scotland and Wales. Northern Ireland, which is at the top of a separate island called Ireland, is politically part of the UK and separate from the country called the Republic of Ireland to its south.

NOTES

[1] As there are many foreigners living in the UK, you could find that the person you ask isn't British, or English etc., at all. Or they could be a mix, such as Scottish-Japanese or English-Australian.

Reading Comprehension

1. The question about nationality for people from the UK
   a. is easy for everyone to answer.
   b. may be easy or difficult, depending on who you ask.
   c. is too hard for anyone's answer to be easily understood.

2. Which statement is NOT true?
   a. Some Scottish and Welsh people don't like the word *Igirisu* to mean Britain.
   b. The terms Britain and the UK mean a collection of countries joined together.
   c. Great Britain is a piece of land which includes England, Scotland, Wales and Ireland.

Chapter 1   The United Kingdom?

Part 2   Why is there no UK football team?

One contribution to the world made by the British, and the English especially, has been the invention of many sports. But how the UK countries and Ireland are represented internationally in the main team sports is complicated, as you can see in the table below.

National teams in the major team sports

Country / Sport	England	Wales	Scotland	Northern Ireland	Republic of Ireland
Football	England	Wales	Scotland	Northern Ireland	Rep. of Ireland
Rugby Union	England	Wales	Scotland	Ireland	Ireland
Cricket	England and Wales		Scotland	Ireland	Ireland
Olympics	Great Britain and Northern Ireland				Ireland

It's even less clear than the table suggests because every few years all the rugby union nations get their players together in one team called the *Lions* to go on tour and play other countries. But such harmony is almost unthinkable in football. All the nations insist they keep separate teams. Only once, in 1958, have all four countries qualified for the World Cup finals, however, so their division no doubt makes them weaker. An Olympic Games rule says there can only be one British team, so often the UK nations don't enter a team at all, and sometimes they enter one organised by the English Football Association, e.g. in 2012 in London.

A cricket match—2 batsmen, some fielders and (wearing the white hat) an umpire.

*R*eading *C*omprehension

3. Which sport is represented by 3 international teams from the two islands of Great Britain and Ireland?

   a. Football.
   b. Rugby union.
   c. Cricket.

Scottish football fans wearing the national dress of kilt and sporran below the blue shirt of the team.

Part 3   Challenges for the UK

The reason for the question mark after the words *United Kingdom* in the title of this chapter is that there are many challenges to the kingdom's unity. One French newspaper has called it the *Disunited Kingdom*.

The social and economic challenges include a bigger gap between rich and poor than in other European countries. In fact, London (where many wealthy Russians, Arabs, Chinese and others live) is Europe's 'richest city', while other parts of England, Wales and Northern Ireland include nine of the ten poorest parts of *northern* Europe[2].

Referendums[3] have been the focus of two of the biggest divisions in national and political life. One was the vote to leave the EU[4]. The other was the vote in 2014 about full independence for Scotland. By a majority of 55% to 45%, people in Scotland voted to stay in the UK. However, the Scottish National Party (SNP) wants another chance for Scotland to become a sovereign nation. The SNP controls the Scottish Parliament, which was opened in 2000, and it has a majority of Scotland's Members of Parliament (MPs) in the UK Parliament in London.

Another division in Scotland is religion. In the biggest city, Glasgow, especially, there is a Protestant-Catholic divide. The issue is even more important in Northern Ireland, which is split between Protestants, who favour union with Britain, and Catholics, who mostly favour joining the Republic of Ireland. Although there is an official, Christian, Protestant, Church of England, headed by the Queen or King, most people in the biggest country aren't religious.

There is also a linguistic challenge in accommodating the significant numbers of immigrants from many different countries into British life. Wales is the one officially bilingual country: about 21% of the population speaks Welsh (though only a few people don't speak English too), and road signs and notices are in both Welsh and English. It's mostly a happy story of a minority language (Welsh) being encouraged by government policy.

The various challenges and complications of Britain certainly make it an interesting place to look at, whether from within or from a distance. ∎

NOTES

[2] See <http://inequalitybriefing.org/brief/briefing-43-the-poorest-regions-of-the-uk-are-the-poorest-in-northern->
[3] 「一般投票、国民投票、レファレンダム」
[4] See Chapter 3

Chapter 1   The United Kingdom?

Reading Comprehension

4. Which of Britain's countries has the widest gap between rich and poor?
   a. England.
   b. Scotland.
   c. Northern Ireland.

5. Which statement is NOT true?
   a. In general, people in England aren't religious.
   b. The idea of Scotland being independent again is still alive.
   c. It's a problem that about a fifth of the population in Wales speaks Welsh.

York Minster, the most important cathedral in the north of England.

Structure Practice

a. Choose the one underlined word or phrase that should be corrected or rewritten. Then change it.

   1. Although the history of the separate countries <u>goes back</u> many hundreds of years, the state of Great Britain is just <u>over</u> 300 years old. It officially <u>begun</u> in 1707, when the Kingdom of Scotland moved its parliament from Edinburgh to <u>join</u> the English parliament in London.

   2. Ireland <u>joined</u> with Great Britain to make the UK in 1801, but in 1922 Ireland <u>splitted</u> between Northern Ireland, <u>which</u> remained part of the UK and the south, which <u>became</u> a separate country.

   3. England had already <u>taken</u> control over Wales <u>formally</u> in the 1500s, too <u>soon</u> for the Welsh dragon to be <u>recognize</u> in the Union Jack, the famous UK flag.

b. Choose the one word or phrase that best completes the sentence.

   4. There's been a lot of emigration and immigration in recent years, but overall Britain's …………………… is increasing: it's now about 65 million.
      a. people   b. population   c. residents   d. birthrate

   5. Recent studies show that one in nine adults in the UK have no ……………… .
      a. examinations   b. documents   c. qualifications   d. tests

Listening Challenge

Listen and fill in the missing words.

1. Scottish and Welsh .... of the British Empire.

2. England is the .... and .... of the four countries; over .... live there.

3. The first official international .... took place between .... and .... in ....

4. Japan's land size is about .... and .... than that of Great Britain.

5. The .... of the UK is about .... that of ....

Going Further (for discussion or research)

1. What is your own image of the UK?

   ....

2. For you, what was the most interesting thing in this chapter?

   ....

3. What is one thing you know about Britain which is not mentioned in this chapter?

   ....

4. What do you think is the biggest challenge facing the UK?

   ....

The railway station at Berwick-upon-Tweed in Northumberland. Because of border changes, the town has been English and Scottish in its history. Now it's in England but many residents feel Scottish.

Chapter 2

Multi-cultural Britain

A dancer at the Notting Hill Carnival, celebrating Caribbean music and culture, in London.

Vocabulary Focus

Match the words in the table with their definition below. Write the word on the line.

colony	immigrant
cosmopolitan	noticeable
harmonious	race

_____race_____ 1. a group of people divided from others according to physical features, e.g., the colour of their skin

_____ 2. going well together, friendly, peaceful

_____ 3. clear to see

_____ 4. someone who has come to live in a country from another country

_____ 5. international, different cultures and countries

_____ 6. a place ruled or controlled by another, more powerful country

Part 1 Background

When Kazuo Ishiguro was awarded the Nobel Prize for Literature in 2017, the Swedish Academy called him "the English author". Although he was born in Nagasaki, he has lived in England since the age of 5, and is just one example of a successful immigrant. In sport, over 80 black or mixed race footballers have played for England[1], even though the first one wasn't picked for the team until 1978[2]. It was a news event then, but now, half the team are often BME[3] players.

These days the word *cosmopolitan* is often used to describe London, and British society is often described as multicultural, but the history of Britain shows immigrants have long played an important role in British life. One example from the 1850s is the half Jamaican, half Scottish nurse Mary Seacole. Born in Jamaica, she made her way to the Crimean War where she bravely nursed wounded and dying British soldiers. Until a few years ago, Florence Nightingale, a white nurse from an upper class English family, also in Crimea in the middle of the 19th century, was much better known. Now, though, Seacole's value is recognized again and her life is taught in schools.

NOTES
[1] Most were born in England.
[2] His name was Viv Anderson, a right back.
[3] BME = Black or Minority Ethnic

 Mary Seacole

*R*eading *C*omprehension

1. Which statement is true?
   a. Non-white people, born to non-British parents, sometimes represent England.
   b. The Nobel Prize committee thought Kazuo Ishiguro was born in England.
   c. Over 80 black or mixed race footballers played for England in 1978.

2. The fact that Mary Seacole is taught in schools shows that
   a. London is a cosmopolitan city.
   b. she was a more important nurse than Florence Nightingale.
   c. the role of black minorities in British history is being recognized more than before.

Part 2   64 languages in one school

Can you imagine the capital of Japan having over 37% of its population born abroad? Well, that's the case with London. The population there has been increasing steadily in recent years and is now about 8.7 million. A quarter of its population was not even born in Europe. Not only is London the largest city in Europe; it is also one of the most multi-racial, cosmopolitan cities in the world. One school in north London found that its pupils spoke 64 different languages among them at home. In some schools in London three-quarters of the children only speak English as a second language, and it's over half in some other towns like Leicester and Luton. In fact, the proportion of primary school children in the UK, mainly England[1], who do not speak English as their first language has risen from 13.5% in 2007 to over 20% in 2017. Imagine the challenge for the teachers!

Both at school and as people grow up, there's quite a lot of mixing between races. In fact, nearly one in ten couples are of mixed race.

NOTES
[1] It does not include officially bilingual Wales, and England has had much more recent immigration than Scotland, Northern Ireland or Wales.

*R*eading *C*omprehension

3. About one-fifth of
    a. London's population wasn't born in the UK.
    b. British primary school children can't speak English.
    c. primary school children don't speak English as their first language.

Part 3   Migration

Foreigners have been living in England since the days when it was part of the Roman Empire. In more modern times, London had a Chinatown from the 19th century as the British Empire extended into China. But immigrants with black and brown faces were more noticeable from the 1950s, as the British Empire broke up while Britain itself needed rebuilding after World War II.

Along with people from Ireland, several hundred thousand people from the

West Indies and south Asia moved to Britain to take jobs in transport, the health service and the building industry. At the same time, though, more than a million white people left the UK to start a new life in former colonies such as Australia, New Zealand and Canada.

In some years more people left Britain than entered so the total population remained steady for a long time. But from the late 1990s, a different kind of people movement started. About 500 people were leaving the UK every day to start a new life in younger countries like Australia, or to retire in the sun in Spain or France. However, these emigrants were increasingly outnumbered by the number of immigrants. They came from Europe, especially eastern European countries like Poland, to take jobs in Britain's booming economy. Many more came from India, Pakistan, Bangladesh and Sri Lanka, mostly to join family members. In less than 20 years the population of the UK increased from about 58 million to 65 million.

One of the reasons many people voted to leave the EU was that they wanted less immigration. Some of those who thought there had been too much immigration had been immigrants themselves. One challenge Britain is facing is with some of the younger Muslim population, who often have different values from liberal, non-religious British society.

Generally, however, relations between different groups have mostly been harmonious, and many people agree with the newspaper writer who thought Britain was "lucky" to have so much immigration: first, she wrote, it means people want to live in Britain; second, it makes society livelier; and third, it means Britain's society has been ageing less quickly than Japan's because most immigrants are young and have children. ■

A poster promoting good relations between different races.

*R*eading *C*omprehension

4. Where did most immigrants after the Second World War come from?
    a. Ireland, West Indies, India and Pakistan.
    b. Australia, New Zealand, and Canada.
    c. All the former British colonies.

5. Which of the following is NOT true?
    a. Some people think the country is lucky to have a lot of immigration.
    b. Many older British emigrants leave for sunny European countries.
    c. Immigration is making the British population grow older.

Chapter 2 Multicultural Britain

Structure Practice

a. Choose the one underlined word or phrase that should be corrected or rewritten.

1. London's Notting Hill Carnival, <u>held</u> over three days every August, <u>feature</u> Caribbean and African dance music, and <u>is</u> the second biggest carnival in the world, after Rio de <u>Janeiro's</u>.

2. One in six people now <u>living</u> in England and Wales <u>is</u> non-white, most of <u>which</u> <u>live</u> in cities and big towns.

b. Choose the one word or phrase that best completes the sentence.

3. In the 17th and 18th centuries many French Huguenots, who were Protestants, immigrated to England to escape laws .... their religion in Catholic France.

   a. for b. in favour of c. at d. against

4. The Huguenots brought many skills (for example, in hat making, paper making, silk production and banking) which boosted Britain's industrial revolution but for France's economy were a big ....

   a. loss b. benefit c. surprise d. boost

5. Marks and Spencer, ... one of Britain's most loved and successful chain stores, was started in the 1890s by Michael Marks, a Polish Jewish immigrant.

   a. who is b. who are c. which is d. which are

Listening Challenge

Listen and fill in the missing words.

1. A few years ago, a poster stated proudly that the people who live in London speak .... different languages and follow .... faiths, or ....

2. The British parliament first .... against racial discrimination in 1976 and it was most recently made ....

11

3. Many of England's .... are from .... who came from the Caribbean, while England's cricket .... a few years ago .... to a Muslim family in ....

4. Most British people's .... are Indian, Chinese or Italian, and you .... almost everywhere.

5. While the .... in the UK numbers about .... , British nationals .... number about ....

> The Japanese community in the UK has grown from fewer than 3,000 in 1970 to about 65,000 today. Most live in London, but many Japanese companies have factories in south Wales and Nissan runs the largest car plant in the UK near Sunderland in north-east England.
>
> Having arrived in England with his parents in 1960, Kazuo Ishiguro didn't visit Japan again until 1989, despite his family connections. By then he was 35 and was celebrating the success of his third novel, *The Remains of the Day*.

Going Further (for discussion or research)

1. Do you agree that the UK is "lucky" to have had so much immigration? Why? Why not?

   ....

2. Do you think Japan should allow dual nationality for adults (like Britain does)?

   ....

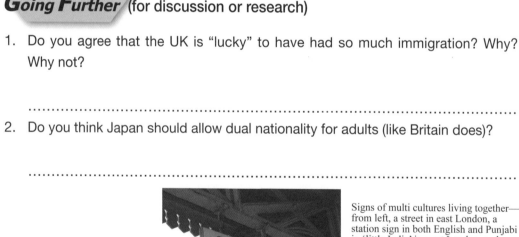

Signs of multi cultures living together—from left, a street in east London, a station sign in both English and Punjabi in 'little India' in west London, and an Islamic mosque next to a Christian church.

Chapter 3

The UK and the EU

A T-shirt made by the EU in Britain to fight the vote to leave the EU. The O in Positive uses the circle of 12 stars of unity from the EU flag.

Vocabulary Focus

Match the words in the table with their definition below. Write the word on the line.

divide	migration
expert	referendum
frustration	revolt

_____expert_____ 1. a person who knows a lot about something

_____ 2. a feeling of anger because you can't do anything about a problem

_____ 3. a rejection of authority by a person or a group

_____ 4. the movement of people from one place to another

_____ 5. separate; break into smaller parts

_____ 6. a vote held by a country to decide on one topic

Part 1 Background: An English Revolt

On 23rd June, 2016, in a referendum, the UK voted to leave the European Union. Both then, and since, the topic has shown a country seriously and evenly divided. The winning margin was only 4%. On a turnout[1] of 72%, 52% voted "Leave" against 48% for "Remain". The topic has divided the British so seriously that there were many reports of family members refusing to talk to each other for months. A famous comedian, who often talks and jokes about current topics, said for the first time large numbers of his audience were walking out of his show because they were so angry at his comments. And this was almost a year after the vote!

The result shocked many British and Europeans, and people elsewhere. They found it hard to believe that a majority of voters in the UK would vote to leave when most political and economic leaders and experts had warned that leaving the EU would be an economic disaster for Britain. In the years before the vote Britain was one of the better-performing economies in the EU, much changed from the country of strikes and industrial decline in the early 1970s when it had joined. But the organisation had changed since then.

In the 1970s it was the European Economic Community. And for the British, it was mainly an economic group to help trade. But most of the other countries wanted greater political and financial union, and in 1993, the EEC changed into the EU. It started the euro, the common currency[2], and also started accepting more members from eastern Europe.

The reasons for the referendum result will be discussed later. But one thing to note is that there were important differences in how various parts of the UK voted. Of the five regions of the UK, three clearly voted to remain—Scotland (by 24%), Northern Ireland (by 12%) and multicultural London (by 20%). Wales voted by a margin of only 5% to leave. But the biggest area in terms of population was England outside London, and that voted by a clear 11% to leave. In effect, the result was largely an English revolt. Interestingly, England outside London was the only area without regional elections and therefore had fewer other ways to let voters have a say on how they were governed[3]. There had been a growing English nationalism for some time, and people who were frustrated that they hadn't been listened to in the years before the referendum expressed their feelings in the vote. Out of the five different areas, England outside London had the biggest population, the highest turnout, and the decisive majority for the winning side.

NOTES

1 「投票率」
2 But the UK and eight other member countries have never joined the euro group.
3 Scotland and Wales have their own Parliaments. Northern Ireland has an Assembly, a kind of parliament. London, with 8.7m voters, chooses its own mayor. There is no English parliament, only the UK Parliament.

Reading Comprehension

1. How was Britain's economy at the time of the referendum?
   a. a disaster   b. quite healthy   c. troubled by strikes

2. Which of the following is true?
   a. All the non-English countries voted to remain.
   b. The clearest vote to remain was in Scotland.
   c. The London area and the rest of England voted in the same way.

Part 2   Brexit: The vote and language

Although in Japan the vote to leave the EU is known as *EU Withdrawal*[4], in Britain the issue is known as *Brexit*. This is a made up word from the first two letters of *Britain* and the word *exit*.

Another word often used in the months following the referendum has been *Remoaners*. This word is made up of *Remain* and *moan*[5]. It always has a bad meaning and is used by pro-Brexit people to criticize those who wanted to stay in the EU and want to change the result of the vote. The Remoaners, or, to use the more neutral word, *Remainers*, argue that there should be another referendum because, first, so many lies about the EU were told by the *Brexiteers* (another made up word referring to the people in favour of Brexit), and second, the vote did not consider the details of the final Brexit agreement with the EU. They also point out that those in favour of leaving the EU had been complaining, or *moaning*, about Britain's involvement in the EU for many years.

The tabloid press campaigned for years against the EU and was delighted by the result.

NOTES

4 「EU 離脱」
5 「愚痴をこぼす、嘆く」

Reading Comprehension

3. Which of the following words is NOT made by joining two other words together?
   a. Brexit	b. Remainer	c. Remoaner

Part 3   So, why did over 17 million people ignore the advice of experts?

First, there was a frustration among many people that their problems had not been taken seriously for too long. After the financial crisis in 2008, bankers and the richest in society seemed to be getting richer while most people saw their standard of living falling. Many of the jobs being created were poor quality with low pay and few career prospects. Then in 2009 an expenses scandal involving MPs disgusted the public. People saw those at the top of society doing well out of the current conditions, including EU membership, and by 2016 were in the mood *not* to follow the advice of economic experts, business and political leaders.

Another big reason given by voters to leave was immigration. Although no one argues there shouldn't be any immigration, in the early 2000s more people expressed a wish for less. Between 1998 and 2010, there was a *net*[6] addition to the UK (mostly England) population of 3.6 million foreign born immigrants, both from Europe and the rest of the world. The numbers continued to flow in until the record number, in 2015, of 330,000 additional people in one year. Many people complained that their towns were struggling with the increase. They said there weren't enough places to live, not enough places for school children, and an increasing pressure on the National Health Service.

Only part of this increased immigration was due to EU membership and its freedom of movement rules allowing EU citizens to live and work where they wanted. Most political and business leaders were relaxed about immigration. But those running the campaign for Britain to leave blamed EU rules and fought the referendum with the clever slogan *Take Back Control*. They argued that Britain should be able to control who entered the country and make its own laws without being told what to do by the EU. The pro-Brexit campaign was led by two effective leaders, whereas the government leaders arguing for "Remain" failed to highlight the positive things the EU had done for Britain. Their weak message was basically, 'we don't like the EU much, but it's too scary to leave.' It was summed up in the phrase *Project Fear*. It's not surprising more people found *Take Back Control* more attractive.

But how much control Britain will get back from Brexit remains to be seen. The future will also show how much truth there was in the mostly economic warnings of *Project Fear*. ∎

NOTES ─────────────
6 The difference between the numbers of immigrants and emigrants.

*R*eading *C*omprehension

4. What wasn't a reason why people voted for Brexit?
   a. Frustration with Britain's political leaders and economic experts.
   b. The standard of care in the National Health Service.
   c. The high levels of net immigration.

5. What did pro-Brexit people 'think' they were voting for?
   a. No immigration.
   b. A change of government.
   c. More control over their lives.

*S*tructure *P*ractice

a. Choose the one underlined word or phrase that should be corrected or rewritten. Then change it.

   1. Britain joined the European Economic Community in 1973 along with Ireland and Denmark, bring membership of the EEC to nine countries. By 2016, 28 countries were members of the European Union, a larger and more politically unified organisation.

   2. A big change in recent years has been the large number of citizens of other EU countries living in the UK. More than 3.5 million had lived in Britain, and most are working.

b. Choose the one word or phrase that best completes the sentence.

   3. The biggest increase in foreign-born UK .... was among people from Poland whose numbers jumped from 94,000 in 2004 to over 900,000 in 2016.

      a. citizens   b. nationalities   c. residents   d. workers

4. Around the time of the Brexit vote, 1.2 million people who _____ in Britain were living in other EU countries, with Spain easily the most popular.

   a. born	b. was born	c. were born	d. were not born

5. One reason Northern Ireland probably voted for "Remain" is because it is the only part of the UK with a .... border with the EU, and membership has meant an easy movement between that country and Ireland in the south.

   a. controlled	b. land	c. sea	d. secure

Listening Challenge

Listen and fill in the missing words.

1. The regions of Britain .... had the .... in the referendum.

2. The UK was one of .... out of 28 members of the EU which has .... the Euro for its currency.

3. In general, ..., who remembered life before EU membership, were much more .... the EU than younger voters*.

4. Being a member of the EU has meant .... laws which govern the EU ....

5. For example, the EU .... Britain to .... who committed less serious crimes ....

NOTES ────────────────
*Some younger people feared losing the right to live and work anywhere in Europe, which EU membership gives all its citizens.

Chapter 4

Tea

An afternoon cream tea: tea and a scone, with jam and cream.

Vocabulary Focus

Match the words in the table with their definition below. Write the word on the line.

advertise	kettle
custom	meal
interval	plentiful

<u> advertise </u> 1. tell people about a product to encourage them to buy it

_____ 2. food eaten at a time like breakfast, lunch or dinner

_____ 3. plenty, a lot of something

_____ 4. a kitchen item used to boil water

_____ 5. a short break between parts of a game or concert

_____ 6. a usual way of behaving in a particular society

19

Welcome to Britain

Part 1 Background

It is well known that tea is Britain's unofficial national drink. But the history of tea shows how the customs of a country can change. England has been a country for more than a thousand years, but tea didn't become a popular drink until the middle of the 18th century.

The first recorded request for tea in English was made in 1615 by an English trader working in Japan. From the island of Hirado[1], he wrote to one of his colleagues who was working in Kyoto and asked him to send "only the best sort of chaw." Notice how close that last word is to the Japanese or Chinese word today. Over the next century the word for the drink in English moved from *tcha* and *tay*, to *tee* and finally to *tea*.

Tea was first brought to Europe by the Dutch[2], Portuguese and French. It first arrived in England in 1658, when it was advertised as both a delicious drink and one that was good for health. But tea took nearly a hundred years to become popular, partly because high taxes made it so expensive and partly because it was hard to get. Until the mid-1700s, therefore, it was a luxury item for the upper class.

'British tea' now is usually made with black tea and drunk with milk, and often sugar, added. However, this particular drink also shows a change in social customs. The heavier types of tea, like Ceylon and Assam, only became more common than Chinese teas, which are usually drunk without milk, in late 19th century Britain. That was when India, Sri Lanka and Kenya, countries then ruled by Britain, started producing so much tea that it became cheap and plentiful.

NOTES
[1] Hirado is about two hours north of Nagasaki.
[2] Dutch = the people from, or the language spoken in, Holland, the Netherlands (オランダ)

*R*eading *C*omprehension

1. For its first 100 years, tea in Britain was a luxury only for the upper class because
    a. it was brought back from China by the Dutch, Portuguese and French.
    b. it cost a lot and not many shops had it.
    c. it didn't taste good.

2. The information above shows how a country's traditions
    a. can change over time.
    b. take 100 years to change.
    c. stay the same.

Part 2   Tea, the social oil

Unlike some other countries, including Japan, there is no formal tea ceremony in Britain. But more tea is drunk per head in Britain than anywhere else and a kettle is probably the most important item in the kitchen. That's because British tea should be made with water freshly boiled and still boiling, not the 80–90°C acceptable for green tea.

As oil is to an engine, tea is to many British people's daily social life. There's even an old, popular song which says everything 'stops for tea'. Many activities do: people stop work to enjoy their tea break in mid afternoon, when even international cricket matches take a 20 minute break called the 'tea interval'.

The English had a trading company at Hirado in Kyushu for ten years at this site (1613–1623).

Phrases like "I'll put the kettle on", "Would you like some tea?" and "Let's have a nice cuppa"[3] are common in real life as well as in literature and dramas. The kettle is often put on when someone is feeling bad about something, or people arrive somewhere after a journey. In an essay about making tea George Orwell[4] wrote that 'a nice cup of tea' was "a comforting phrase".

NOTES

[3] Cuppa is short for 'cup of tea'.
[4] George Orwell was one of Britain's most famous 20th century writers. He wrote *Animal Farm* and *1984*.

Reading Comprehension

3. In Britain, tea is often made
    a. to welcome people in formal ceremonial occasions.
    b. so people can use the kettle in their kitchen.
    c. to help people feel better.

George Orwell, 1903–50.

Part 3   Meals with tea: afternoon tea and high tea

Tea is popular at all levels of society. High Tea is a meal, often including meat or fish and bread and butter, eaten at around 6pm especially in northern England and Scotland. The meal is usually called tea and it may or may not include the drink tea! People who regularly *eat* tea call a cooked meal at lunchtime 'dinner'. They also often eat a snack like sandwiches later in the evening.

Afternoon tea is lighter than high tea. It consists of small sandwiches and cakes, eaten between 3 and 4pm. When scones, served with cream and jam, are provided it is also called a cream tea. Great care is taken in the presentation of the best afternoon teas and they are usually found in expensive hotels and specialist tea shops. Such high class surroundings seem appropriate because afternoon tea was started in the mid-1800s by an upper-class woman called Anna, the Duchess of Bedford. She began inviting her friends to join her in this light meal as they felt hungry between lunch, which was light, and the main meal, dinner.

People in modern Britain don't eat afternoon or cream teas in their *daily* lives. But they do enjoy their tea breaks—often drinking their tea from a large mug, accompanied by biscuits or a chocolate snack. Tea drinking has declined in recent years as people have turned to fruit juice, herbal infusions and coffee, but tea is still the most popular, still the national drink. ■

Reading Comprehension

4. What is High Tea?
   a. A meal like an early dinner.
   b. A fashionable social custom.
   c. Sandwiches eaten late in the evening.

5. Which of the following is NOT true?
   a. Tea's popularity in recent years has been challenged by other drinks.
   b. Even now, afternoon teas like Anna's are enjoyed by most British people nearly everyday.
   c. People often eat biscuits (or cookies, in American English) while they take their tea breaks.

Tea at a high class hotel restaurant.

Chapter 4 Tea

Structure Practice

a. Choose the one word or phrase that best completes the sentence.

1. Tea .... the English language. For example, the phrase *It's not really my cup of tea* means *I don't like it much*.
   a. has influenced   b. is like   c. has ruined   d. has created

2. The English novelist Anthony Burgess once wrote, "The best thing to do, when you've got a dead body and it's your husband's on the kitchen floor and you don't know what to do about it, is to .... a good strong cup of tea."

   a. make your neighbour   c. make yourself
   b. drink yourself   d. go to a vending machine and buy

b. Choose the one underlined word or phrase that should be rewritten. Correct it.

3. Tea drinking <u>helped</u> the pottery makers in England to <u>develop</u> their business. British people <u>preferred</u> cups with handles to the straight cups which had been <u>brung</u> back from China.

4. Milk first or last has often been a topic <u>for</u> discussion. Milk first protects a delicate cup <u>to</u> boiling water, but most people say it's better to put the milk <u>in</u> last so you can more easily judge how much to add <u>to</u> your tea.

5. One recent <u>win</u> of the <u>best</u> tea shop <u>of the</u> year award was Juri's, a tea shop <u>run by</u> a Japanese family in the Cotswold town of Winchcombe in central England.

Juri (below, left) and her parents in their tea shop on the main street at Winchcombe near Cheltenham.

Welcome to Britain

Listening Challenge

Listen and fill in the missing words.

1. Americans changed their main .... to .... as a patriotic act during the American War of Independence.

2. The .... after some Americans in Boston in 1773 threw boxes of tea into the sea instead of paying the new .... which the British ....

3. These days, although .... is drunk in Ireland, Australia and ...., in the United States tea is most often ....

4. Experts agree that loose leaf tea results in a .... , but .... of tea drunk in Britain these days is made with the more convenient .... , originally ....

5. As .... helped to .... the British .... of drinking so much tea, according to the UK Tea Council[5], the irony is that the .... finally made a .... to Britain's tea industry.

NOTES
[5] See www.tea.co.uk.

Going Further (for discussion or research)

1. What are the similarities and differences of the Japanese and British tea drinking customs?

   ....

2. Very little tea is grown in the UK. Which Japanese traditions or customs are based on something imported?

   ....

Chapter 5

Social class

A famous BBC TV comedy making fun of social class. Comic actors play the upper class (left), the middle class and the lower class (right).

Vocabulary Focus

Match the words in the table with their definition below. Write the word on the line.

aristocrat	forbidden
conscious	reality TV
embarrassment	spectator

conscious   1. aware, noticing

_____ 2. not allowed

_____ 3. television programmes showing real people, not actors, in dramatic or humorous situations

_____ 4. someone who watches something like a sports game or event

_____ 5. a member of a family of high social rank with a title, e.g., the Duke of Westminster

_____ 6. a feeling of shyness or shame

Part 1 Background

In 1990 the new British Prime Minister[1] said he wanted to create "a classless society." To some extent, his own story showed class mattered less than before: he had risen from an ordinary, lower class family to become the head of the government. But although most people agree in surveys that class matters less in British life than it used to, it's still significant and sense of class—'class consciousness'—remains strong. One serious reason is concern that Britain has become more unequal in the last 30 years or so. Research shows that the class you're brought up in will probably make a difference in how your life will proceed.

NOTES
[1] John Major, Prime Minister and leader of the Conservative Party 1990–97.

Class isn't only about money

Former Prime Minister John Major.

Another reason for class consciousness is that your class isn't shown simply by how much money you have. British footballers who suddenly become rich are usually still working class. It's possible to be upper class and not rich, but your family would have been wealthy at least in the past. Being upper class depends more on how long money has been in your family: a few years ago one aristocrat famously looked down on a successful, wealthy politician because he'd "had to buy his own furniture." This comment meant the politician had become rich recently through business: real upper class people usually had old, but high quality, furniture handed down from one generation to the next.

More than income, though, your class is shown by your attitude to things, such as education (if you worry about your child's education, you're middle class), or organic vegetables (if you buy them you're middle class). Also, by the way you speak (discussed in the language chapter); what sport you play; what you watch on TV; how tall or healthy you are (the higher social classes are usually taller and can expect to live longer, healthier lives); even by how many clothes you wear!

Reading Comprehension

1. Which statement is true?
   a. Class isn't relevant in modern Britain.
   b. Class is relevant in Britain today, but less than it used to be.
   c. Class is still the biggest factor which determines the course of your life.

2. The class people belong to is shown by
   a. just how rich they are.
   b. where they buy their furniture.
   c. their wealth and a complicated set of attitudes to life.

> There are about 7 different classes: upper class (only 1 or 2%), upper-middle, middle-middle, lower-middle, skilled working class, unskilled working-class, and an underclass of long-term unemployed. Although most people are really somewhere in the middle, Britain is unusual in that about half the population claim to be working class. They think it sounds better.
>
> Some academics say the traditional terms are out of date and invented seven new classes. For example, in place of a traditional upper class, they have an Elite class, which is about 6% of the population. You can find which class you're in at this website: http://www.bbc.com/news/magazine-22000973

Part 2   Class isn't always serious

People usually look down most on the class just below them as 'common'. However, people lower down the social scale criticize the upper classes for being 'posh[2]'. But although class does create divisions in British (especially English) society, it should not be taken *too* seriously. Or perhaps the way it is treated shows that it is just a normal part of British life. In Britain, people joke about everything, often as a way to cover their social embarrassment, which means people not feeling comfortable with each other. Class is both a cause of social embarrassment and a source of humour. Indeed, some television comedy programmes and dramas have made fun of people who are too conscious of their position on the social class scale. But especially through education and marriage, people can move class so they are not fixed in a particular place or forbidden to do anything because of the class to which they belong.

NOTES
[2] posh 「上流階級の、しゃれた、気取った」

Reading Comprehension

3. Which statement is NOT true?
   a. It's possible for an English person to move up the social scale.
   b. In England, class is the one topic that is too serious to laugh about.
   c. Because of class differences, people in England sometimes don't feel comfortable with each other.

Part 3 Sport, TV, drinks, and clothes all show your social class

In England class is often related to sport. Rugby union is mainly played by middle class boys because it's only played at schools which cost a lot of money, whereas football is played by working class or lower-middle class children. But watching Premier League football live now costs a lot of money and the stadiums are much more comfortable than they used to be, so lots of spectators now are from the middle classes. Tennis and golf are middle class, but racing[3] is mostly popular with the upper-class and working-class.

Comedy programmes on television are usually enjoyed by people from all classes, but many programmes are popular with different classes: reality TV shows and soaps with the working class, nature programmes and documentaries with the middle classes. The BBC is often praised for its quality but also criticized for being 'too middle-class' in its view of the world.

Wine has become more popular in general in recent years but it is still regarded mainly as middle- or upper-class, whereas mass-produced beer is working class. Middle class beer drinkers prefer 'real ale', which is made the old-fashioned way, without the use of carbon dioxide. How people dress often depends on their job, which may or may not tell you which class they belong to. What is interesting is that working class people usually wear fewer clothes, especially in winter. If you see someone (especially a younger man) wearing a thick coat, scarf, or gloves, the person will probably be upper- or middle-class. In most cases it is not because working class people cannot afford these items, but because they think that wearing so many clothes is not manly. The colder the place, for example Newcastle in the north east of England, the fewer clothes they wear! ∎

NOTES

[3] Horse-racing, but always known simply as 'racing'.

Chapter 5 Social class

*R*eading *C*omprehension

Playing rugby.

4. Someone who is keen on football and horse-racing, and drinking regular beer, and watching reality TV, and wears light clothes in cold weather is almost certainly
   a. working class.
   b. middle class.
   c. upper class.

5. Someone who plays tennis, and mostly drinks wine, and watches documentaries on BBC TV, and wears a scarf and gloves in cold weather is almost certainly
   a. working class.
   b. middle class.
   c. upper class.

*S*tructure *P*ractice

a. Choose the one underlined word or phrase that should be corrected or rewritten. Then change it.

1. Have the right personal contacts still helps people get good jobs, so 'who you know' is still considered more important than 'what you know', giving an advantage to people in the higher classes.

2. Until the 1960s English cricket teams were divided into 'gentlemen' and 'players'. The formal were upper or middle class amateurs, not paid because they already had enough money. The latter were professional cricketers from working or lower middle class families.

b. Choose the one word or phrase that best completes the sentence.

3. In England, rugby union (played by teams of 15 players) is mostly southern and middle class, ………… rugby league (played by teams of 13) is a working-class game popular in the north.

   a. despite   b. whereas   c. because   d. although

4. In Wales, rugby union is played and watched by all classes, ………… even there, more people play and watch football.

   a. despite   b. whereas   c. because   d. although

5. Although anyone might buy underwear at Marks and Spencer department store, only middle class people …………… often buy food there. It's too expensive for the working class but not special enough for the upper class.

   a. can   b. may   c. should   d. would

Listening Challenge

Listen and fill in the missing words.

1. The British ………… ………… does ………… ………… people in certain positions like the caste system in ………….

2. It is true, however, that from an ……………… ………… people in the higher social classes have ……………… , nutritional and ………… ……………… over those further down the scale.

3. In a recent survey, the number one item which showed someone was middle class was ………… a ……………… ……………… ………… ………….

4. In Scotland, class is less important than an interest in nationalism and education, but Glasgow (the ……………… city) is ……………… working class and Edinburgh (the …………… city) middle class.

5. The Wimbledon …………… tournament, Lords, the home of …………… , and the Ascot …………… and ……………… event are middle- or upper-class.

Going Further (for discussion or research)

1. What do you think of the British class system?

   ………………………………………………………………………………………………

2. How conscious are you of class differences in your own life?

   ………………………………………………………………

   ………………………………………………………………

Wimbledon tennis championships take place on grass at the All England Club in south London.

Chapter 6

Schools and education

Schoolboys wearing uniform on their way to school.

Vocabulary Focus

Match the words in the table with their definition below. Write the word on the line.

compulsory	im- (prefix)
discipline	priority
grade	underclass

<u>underclass</u> 1. a group of people who are poor and have little hope of improving their situation

_____ 2. something you have to do, like a subject at school

_____ 3. a score or mark which shows your level of achievement

_____ 4. the most important thing which needs to be done

_____ 5. not - (at the beginning of a word)

_____ 6 making people behave well or obey rules and punishing them if they don't do that

31

Part 1 Background

Britain and Japan have something in common about this topic: it's considered too important to be left to teachers. Politicians in the government and officials in the education ministries make education policies which change every few years. When one policy seems to work imperfectly, something else is tried. In 1997 the new British Prime Minister[1] said his priority in government was, "education, education, education". But the only generally agreed achievement his government managed was a continuing increase in the number of school-leavers going on to university. This was partly a result of a larger number of places available and partly a result of better grades in the school exams taken by 18-year-olds. But not everyone agreed these better grades were due to better schooling. Many people argued the tests were getting easier, or that the grades were increasingly awarded for work that could be retaken, several times if necessary, rather than for a final exam.

One thing seems certain: in terms of education Britain is increasingly a place of the 'haves' and the 'have-nots'. In some areas there are excellent schools, from which most of the children go on to enter top universities. But in other areas too many children leave school with few or no qualifications. Many become part of a long-term, NEET[2] underclass.

Most schools and teachers are trying their best, but many problems come from home, starting at an early age. Some children start school without knowing their own name and recent national tests showed that a third of 11-year-olds had a reading age of 7 or below. Discipline is often lacking, at home and at school.

NOTES
[1] Tony Blair. He was PM and leader of the Labour Party until 2007.
[2] NEET is short for: Not in Education, Employment or Training.

Tony Blair,
Prime Minister 1997–2007.

*R*eading *C*omprehension

1. Which statement is NOT true?
   a. Education policies for schools often change.
   b. Education is always the government's main priority.
   c. More 18 year olds have been doing well enough to enter university.

2. Why is Britain in education terms a place of 'haves' and 'have-nots'?
   a. Some children can go to school, but others cannot.
   b. Many rich foreign children become part of the NEET underclass.
   c. Children do very well at school in some areas, but many fail badly in others.

Part 2 Britain's school system

By law, children have to be in education from the age of 5. That doesn't mean they have to go to school: an increasing number of mostly middle-class parents are choosing to educate their children at home. That's always been legal in Britain.

Most children do go to school and about 92% of those are in the *state*[3] system. That means the government pays and it's free to go to school. From age 5 to 11 pupils go to *primary* school; from 11 to 16 or 18, they go to *secondary* school. There are also colleges for 16 to 18 year olds. Most schools are mixed[4], but there are some which are single-sex. Almost all schools have their own uniform. A new development is the opening of more than 20 'free' schools. These are in the state system but controlled by parents, not the local government.

You might imagine British schools are like Hogwarts, from the Harry Potter films. Well, you'd find something like that only in the *independent*, or private, system. And even then, until the age of 16, *boarding* schools (where pupils live during term time) are single-sex. Not all pupils at independent schools are boarders; some are day pupils. Many of these schools offer smaller class sizes, highly qualified teachers, beautiful grounds and wonderful facilities. They're also expensive, costing 25,000 to 35,000 pounds a year.

NOTES
[3] state = government-run
[4] Mixed means for boys and girls; *co-ed* is an American term.

Reading Comprehension

3. Which statement is true?
   a. All children must attend school from the age of 5.
   b. Most children go to primary and secondary state schools.
   c. All independent schools are just like Hogwarts in the Harry Potter films.

Children and their teacher at a primary school in London.

Part 3 Britain's testing culture and challenges

One thing pupils and teachers are agreed on: they're all under pressure from the government to succeed. Education in British schools has often been about encouraging pupils' original thought. But since the 1980s different governments have said it's more important to have core, compulsory subjects which pupils are strictly tested on all through their school years. Schools are judged according to how their pupils perform. They are ranked in published tables and if a school doesn't reach certain targets it can be put under the control of a stricter headteacher or even closed. Many teachers say they can't educate pupils so much as 'teach to the tests' or use a 'spoon-feeding approach'. That means they just give them information for the tests, like spoon-feeding food to a baby.

Many teachers and pupils have argued too many tests add unnecessary stress. Even the politicians accepted this and the national tests at age 14 were dropped.

So, what and when are the tests? Look at this graphic:

Ages 5, 7, 11: Tests in core subjects → Age 16: GCSEs → Age 17: AS-levels → Age 18: A2-levels

At 5 and 7 the core subjects are reading, writing, and use of numbers. At age 11 basic science is added. At age 16, all pupils must take GCSEs in English, maths and science, but can choose their other subjects. Most do seven or eight subjects in all. Popular ones include design and technology, history, French, geography, and information technology (that is, using computers).

The second group of national exams at secondary school is called A-levels, 'A' meaning Advanced. Pupils study three or four subjects in depth over two years. If pupils pass the first year of AS-level work, they continue to study for the A2-levels at 18. If they pass these and get high enough grades, they can go on to university. When the A-level results come out in August it's an anxious time for school-leavers, their parents, and their teachers. ∎

*R*eading *C*omprehension

4. Which statement is true?
   a. Teachers say their pupils are like babies.
   b. Schools and pupils are under stress to do well.
   c. Each pupil's test results are published in a ranking table.

5. Each pupil must take national tests in both English and science at ages:
   a. 5, 7, 11, 16, 17
   b. 7, 11, 16
   c. 11 and 16

Chapter 6 Schools and education

*S*tructure *P*ractice

a. Choose the one underlined word or phrase that should be corrected or rewritten. Then change it.

1. The school-leaving age was risen from 16 to 18* in an attempt to reduce the number of teenage NEETS.

2. There's a huge difference between the best state secondary schools and the worse. Because children are supposed to attend a school near their home, some families even buy a house in an area where the schools are known to be good.

3. That kind of house-buying drives up local property prices and mean such schools are full of children from richer families. Meanwhile, the poorer schools often get worse.

b. Choose the one word or phrase that best completes the sentence.

4. Some new school teachers start teaching as a second .... in early middle age after giving up their first.

   a. career   b. job   c. try   d. work

5. The government tries to encourage people to move into teaching; recently it's been .... former soldiers for school teaching.

   a. encouraging   b. teaching   c. testing   d. training

   NOTES
   *The government changed the law in 2015.

*L*istening *C*hallenge

Listen and fill in the missing words.

1. The standard assessment .... in the .... are pronounced informally as .... , Sats, whereas in .... the school tests are called ....

2. In .... , schoolchildren do exams called 'standard grade' .... , and 'highers' and '................ highers' at the ages of 17 and 18, not ....

3. No one knows .... children are .... -schooled because you don't have to register, but estimates range from ......-thousand to ....

4. Some British schoolchildren .... and take .... classes after school, but there aren't so many .... as in Japan.

5. Another .... is that in Britain schools give more .... , but there aren't any .... , or *juku*.

Going Further (for discussion or research)

1. What do you think is one good point the British system has which Japan doesn't have?

   ....

2. What is one good point Japan's system has which Britain doesn't have?

   ....

3. Do you think English should be a compulsory subject in Japanese schools? Why (not)?

   ....

4. Which is the best way to assess the progress of pupils and students (tests, or what else)?

   ....

How do school students apply for university?

In Britain people who want to enter university apply to UCAS (pronounced You-cas), not directly to a university or college. UCAS is a central office which deals with the applications. Applicants make a list of 5 courses they would like to take. The universities reply with an offer or rejection. If applicants have several offers, they keep two choices. If the results of their A-levels or Highers (in Scotland) are good enough they can enter their first choice university. Applicants whose grades are not good enough when they receive their results in August can apply to UCAS again to find a place through 'clearing'. Clearing is a process by which UCAS helps match applicants and places available at different universities round the country.

Chapter 7

University students and higher education

Kings College, Cambridge University, was founded in 1441 by King Henry VI. The chapel is famous for its architecture and its choir.

Vocabulary Focus

Match the words in the table with their definition below. Write the word on the line.

employer	graduate
enthusiasm	socialize
explosion	tuition

__tuition__   1. teaching about a subject, often at university

_____ 2. a great desire to do something you like doing

_____ 3. a large, quick increase

_____ 4. meet friends for activities away from work or studies

_____ 5. a company (or person) which provides work

_____ 6. successfully complete a course

37

Part 1 Background

The UK has long been famous for its university education. The two oldest and best known are the Universities of Oxford and Cambridge, both about an hour from London, which were founded in the 12th and 13th centuries. They are still ranked in the best five universities in the world. Of the 14 Prime Ministers of the UK since 1945, eleven graduated from Oxford. Researchers and professors with close connections to Cambridge University have won more Nobel Prizes than people from any other institution in the world.

A lot of universities and other colleges were set up in the late 19th century and some more in the 20th. Academic study after high school is often called 'higher education'. There are now 165 higher education institutions in the UK, most of them in England. The two biggest universities[1] are both in the city of Manchester, where there are more than 75,000 students. Other big student cities include Leeds, Bristol and London, but the numbers of students compared to the total populations make students more noticeable in Oxford and Cambridge.

Gap years

One big difference between Britain and Japan is that more than a quarter of UK students have had a year's break between school and university. Taking a *gap year*[2], which people spend travelling round the world and/or doing voluntary work, has become increasingly popular. The benefits include students showing more enthusiasm about studying after time doing something different. It's good for getting a job, too. Employers often prefer graduates with experience of life away from school. But the UK and Japan have this in common: when the economy is doing badly, a lot of graduates find it hard to get a job.

NOTES
[1] The University of Manchester and Manchester Metropolitan University.
[2] See www.gapyear.com for details on what young people do.

Traditional Oxford University buildings blend in with the modern town.

Reading Comprehension

1. Which do you think is true from the information above?
    a. The Universities of Oxford and Cambridge are about 500 years old.

b. Cambridge is famous for scientific research and Oxford for politicians who went there.
c. If you travel in a triangle from London to Oxford, on to Cambridge and back to London, it will take about an hour.

2. Why is taking a gap year thought to be a good thing?
   a. More than a quarter of British students do voluntary work.
   b. Travelling round the world has become increasingly popular.
   c. Students enjoy themselves and it can improve their chance of getting a good job later.

Part 2   Today: Social change

In addition to the number of gappers[3], there are two sets of figures which have grown in recent years—how many students there are, and how much it costs to be one. First, let's consider the explosion in student numbers, a clear social change. In 1980 only about one young person in 10 studied in higher education. Ten years later one in 5 young people were going to university or college. The Labour government which came to power in 1997 set a target for 2010 of one in two. That is, it aimed for 50% of young people to be studying in higher education. When Labour lost power that year it also had to admit the target had not been reached— but not by much. By the end of the noughties[4] nearly 500,000 young people, or around 45%, were at university or another kind of college. Actually, among females, it was 50%!

NOTES
[3] gappers = people who take a gap year
[4] The word *noughties* comes from *nought* which means zero. As there are noughts in every year between 2000 and 2009, the decade is now often referred to as the noughties. For humorous reasons, too, people like the way it sounds like *naughty*.

Reading Comprehension

3. Complete this table with the correct figures.

Year	1980	1990	2010
% of young people as students			

Part 3 Paying to be a student

The second big increase in figures is the cost of tuition. When few people went to university, tuition was free. It was paid for by the government which means, of course, taxpayers. But as so many people started going to university the government decided the cost was too great. Fees were first introduced in the late 1990s and were raised over the next few years. When the new government announced in 2010 that universities could charge a maximum of 9,000 pounds a year, big demonstrations were held to protest this decision, but the government refused to back down.

Student life

So, once at college, how do British students spend their time? Not so differently from Japanese students. They study, go to lectures and seminars, write papers, take exams and join clubs. Doing a part-time job is normal, but more common in the summer holidays than during the term. Students also socialize with their friends. The last is perhaps what they value most. A lot of the time they do it while drinking beer! Each university campus has several bars so they don't have to go far to drink, but usually they prefer to drink in pubs in the city or town. Of course, drinking costs money, living accommodation, food and books cost money and now tuition costs a lot of money. Therefore, it's not surprising that most students say their biggest problem is "money." But most manage to continue as students because banks give them a loan which they pay back when they start working. This has resulted, though, in the average student graduating with a debt of more than 50,000 pounds. ■

One of Britain's biggest banks, HSBC, welcoming new students to Sheffield University. Banks make big efforts to get students as new customers.

*R*eading *C*omprehension

4. Which of the following is NOT true? The government says:
   a. the growth in student numbers is a good thing for society.
   b. its education budget will pay for students' university fees.
   c. it won't change its mind about the latest increase in tuition fees.

Chapter 7   University students and higher education

5. What is something many British students do which most Japanese students don't do?
   a. attend lectures and write papers.
   b. borrow money from a bank.
   c. drink alcohol.

Structure Practice

a. Choose the one word or phrase that should be corrected. Then correct it.

1. Critics of the government argue that <u>as</u> Britain is <u>short of</u> electricians and plumbers and other non-academic skilled workers, it <u>is</u> better for everyone if more people trained for that kind of job and fewer young people <u>went</u> to university.

2. Students from abroad already pay <u>more the</u> new tuition fees <u>for</u> British students, and the government says fees for overseas students <u>won't</u> go up, or not <u>by much</u>.

3. Some people predict the <u>popular</u> of gap years will <u>go down</u> as more students will <u>have to</u> save more to pay for the <u>tuition</u> fees they will have to pay at university.

b. Choose the one word or phrase that best completes the sentence.

4. .... in a university dormitory in their first year, then move into a house or flat to share with friends they have made for their second and third years.

   a. Almost students live   c. Almost of all students lived
   b. Most students live   d. Mostly students have lived

5. Larger numbers of mature students and part-time students, ... students from the usual 18-22 age group, mean there are now more students in higher education than ever before.

   a. in place of   c. so that the
   b. as well as   d. after all the

Listening Challenge

Listen and fill in the missing words.

1. Most British students study at a .... institution away from their .... and develop .... from their family.

2. Most .... and .... at British universities last ....

3. University clubs are usually called .... or 'socs' for short, so, for example, ... DramSoc.

4. For many British people .... and .... are most .... for staging a .... on the River Thames in London each April.

5. The .... UK university is St. Andrews[4], a .... on the east coast of Scotland, also known as the .... of .... It was founded in the 15th century.

NOTES

[4] St. Andrews is where Prince William met his wife Kate. They both studied History of Art, although he finally graduated with a degree in geography.

Going Further (for discussion or research)

1. How did you choose which universities to apply for?

   ....

2. How and why did you choose your main subject to study?

   ....

3. What do you think of the idea of taking a 'gap year' between school and university?

   ....

Chapter 8

Women in society

Vocabulary Focus

Match the words in the table with their definition below. Write the word on the line.

anti-social	medicine
glass ceiling	millionaire
maternity leave	profession

profession 1. a kind of job for which formal qualifications are needed

_____ 2. treatment for illness

_____ 3. a very rich person who has at least a million pounds or dollars

_____ 4. the time a mother is allowed away from work when she has her baby

_____ 5. annoying or upsetting to other people

_____ 6. attitudes or traditions (not official rules) that stop women getting the best jobs in a company

Part 1   Background

In 1865 someone called E. Garrett came top of a national British exam for students who wanted to become a doctor. The men in charge of the medical profession were shocked to learn that E stood for Elizabeth and that this candidate was a young woman on a nursing course. They refused to accept her and then changed the rules so that other women could not even take the exam.

Garrett's continued determination helped to get the law changed so that from 1876 women were allowed to become doctors. Her story is just one of many stories of women who made a big impression on British society in the 19th century. Another was Julia Margaret Cameron, the portrait photographer.

The monarch, for 64 years, was *Queen* Victoria (1837–1901) but although she had sympathy with the position of women, she was not in favour of women's equality. For example, she didn't believe women should have the right to vote. A group called the 'suffragettes' fought for that in the early years of the 20th century and women were finally allowed to vote on equal terms with men from 1928.

*R*eading *C*omprehension

1. Which of the following is true?
   a. E. Garrett was a man in the medical profession.
   b. E. Garrett helped to get the law changed so that women could become doctors.
   c. Elizabeth Garrett was a candidate for a nursing course in 19th century England.

2. Who were the suffragettes?
   a. A group of women who supported Queen Victoria.
   b. A group of women who were allowed to vote on equal terms with men.
   c. Some women who fought for women to have the right to vote, or 'suffrage'.

Part 2   Today: Ladettes and high academic performance

The word *ladette* entered the language only a few years ago. Ladettes are young women who behave as young men have traditionally been expected to behave—drinking and smoking too much and sometimes being violent. Crimes by teenage girls have increased by more than 20% in recent years. Such behaviour has been blamed on a ladette culture and heavy drinking of alcohol.

Police figures for the arrests of young women for violence are still much

Chapter 8 Women in society

smaller than for young men, but the increased anti-social behaviour of some young women has caused concern. But, at the same time, female students are being praised, especially in contrast to the performance of boys. At school, girls are doing better than boys in A-levels and GCSE exams and the differences after secondary education are even greater. Until Girton College was founded at Cambridge University in 1869, women were not allowed to study at British universities. The chapter on university life explained that there are more students than ever in the UK. The figures also show that now, more women than men go to British universities—50% of young women against 40% of young men. There are even more female students doing what are thought of as 'high status subjects' such as law and medicine. No doubt Elizabeth Garrett would be delighted!

Elizabeth Garrett Anderson

*R*eading *C*omprehension

3. Which of the following is true?
   a. Figures showing the number of young British women drinking lots of alcohol, getting arrested for crimes, getting good grades at school and going to university have all increased.
   b. Figures show that young British women are doing more crimes than young men and until 1969 were not allowed to study at universities in the UK.
   c. Because of a ladette culture, more female students are studying high status subjects at university than men.

Margaret Thatcher, Prime Minister 1979–90.

Part 3   Politics and Business

A woman, Margaret Thatcher, was Britain's longest-serving Prime Minister in modern times (nearly 12 years), but she was nicknamed the Iron Lady and people often joked that she was the strongest 'man' in the government. She also didn't much encourage other women in political life. More positively, the number of female MPs[1] has been steadily increasing. For the first time, in 2017, more than two hundred were elected. In fact, 208 women (32% of the total) were elected. That was 17 more than the election two years before and lifted the UK to 40th in the world rankings. In addition, both the Prime Minister and Home Secretary were

NOTES
[1] MP = Member of Parliament, elected to the House of Commons, the lower house.

female. By contrast, Japan was 164th with only 9.3% of all MPs female.

In the world of business too, women's progress has been mixed. There are few women managers and there is still talk of a 'glass ceiling'. An Equal Pay law was made 40 years ago, but research shows that women on average still get paid about 18% less than men. But there are now more women millionaires than men and an increasing number of businesswomen who have become rich after starting their own company. One of the most successful was Anita Roddick who started the world famous Body Shop at her house.

Other rich businesswomen include Judy Naaké, an ordinary shopworker after leaving school. She started selling St Tropez fake-suntan lotion from the boot of her car in 1995 and sold the company ten years later for 70 million pounds. Sarah Tremellen is another wealthy businesswoman. She started a mail order lingerie business from home while on her maternity leave. The richest 'self-made' woman of all, though, is J.K. Rowling, who wrote the Harry Potter stories. Her given name is Joanne, but her publisher advised her to use the initials J.K. so that boys would not be embarrassed to read the books. A woman using a letter to hide her real first name to be a success—doesn't this sound like E. Garrett more than one hundred years before?! ∎

*R*eading *C*omprehension

4. Complete the table using these figures about women's representation in the lower houses of the British and Japanese parliaments:

| 650 | 465 | 208 | 47 | 164th | 40th | 32% | 10.1% |

Country	World ranking	Percent of women MPs	No. of women MPs	No. of all MPs
U.K.				
Japan				

5. Complete the table to show information about these rich and successful British women:

J.K. Rowling	
	Started The Body Shop, the world-famous cosmetics store
Sarah Tremellen	
	Got rich by selling fake-suntan lotion

Chapter 8   Women in society

*S*tructure *P*ractice

a. Choose the one word or phrase that best completes the sentence.

1. Nearly 70% of all women in Britain now have a paid job, including part-time work, ... less than 50% in 1960.

   a. comparing
   b. compares with
   c. compared to
   d. which is compared with

2. A fictional example of ladette culture is Bridget Jones, a 30-something working woman who smokes and drinks too much and keeps trying to .... while looking for 'Mr. Right'.

   a. lose her weight
   b. lose weight
   c. loose weight
   d. decrease her weight

3. *Bridget Jones' Diary* is a book by Helen Fielding and a movie starring the American actress Renee Zellwegger. Parts of the story are, on purpose, ... the novel *Pride and Prejudice* by Jane Austen, which was first published in 1813.

   a. same as
   b. apart from
   c. similar to
   d. similar from

b. Choose the one underlined word or phrase that should be corrected or rewritten. Correct it.

4. Nearly half of all female students in Britain admit for drinking twice as much in one day as doctors recommend.

5. After finally became accepted by the British medical profession, Elizabeth Garrett set up a women's hospital which is now part of University College Hospital, London.

*L*istening *C*hallenge

Listen and fill in the missing words.

1. British women have often been successful writers. In the 20th .... there was the ...., Agatha Christie, the biggest-selling .... in the world, and the .... writer Beatrix Potter, who

.... of Peter Rabbit.

2. An earlier famous English female writer was Jane Austen whose six .... with clever .... have been filmed in recent years.

3. Some famous contemporary British women are Kate Winslet, the .... , Vivienne Westwood, the .... , and the .... Kate Moss.

4. Some women have got rich in Britain by .... Judges often award .... of .... to women who are divorced by their ....

5. Sandra Davis, a lawyer, said, "I think that there is an investment opportunity in a ...."

Going Further (for discussion or research)

1. Which British woman do you admire and why?

   ....

2. Compare and contrast the life of women in Britain and Japan.

   ....

3. What do you think of the idea that companies should be made, by law, to have a certain number of women managers?

   ....

In September 2017, Jane Austen became the only woman (apart from the Queen) to be shown on a bank note. It was also the first bank note in Britain made from a kind of plastic, which keeps longer than paper, and is harder to copy.

Chapter 9

Science, inventions and business

The BBC (British Broadcasting Corporation) started its television broadcasts here, at Alexandra Palace in 1936. Ally Pally, as the building is nicknamed, is in north London.

Vocabulary Focus

Match the words in the table with their definition below. Write the word on the line.

blade	manufacture
industrialized	patent
inventor	powered by

_____blade_____ 1. long, flat, sometimes sharp, machine part that turns around

_____ 2. to make something, usually in a large amount in a factory

_____ 3. operated by a kind of energy, eg, electricity

_____ 4. having lots of developed industries

_____ 5. someone who makes new things

_____ 6. the official right to be the only person or company allowed to make or sell a product

49

Welcome to Britain

Part 1 Background

Britain has less than 1% of the world's population, but is second only to the United States in the number of influential scientific papers it produces[1]. Over 70 British scientists have won a Nobel Prize for science, and other scientists have won for work done at British universities. Compared to the size of its economy, Britain produces more original science research than any other country in the G7 group of top industrialized nations.

Britain has also produced many unusual people who love to spend their time inventing things. Three everyday items you and your family frequently use are, no doubt, the flushing toilet, the thermos flask, and the vacuum cleaner. All were invented in Britain. So were postage stamps and pencils. In a speech, one of Google's leaders praised Britain for inventing photography, television, and computers.

The interest in inventing machines helped Britain become the first country to have an Industrial Revolution, and has continued to the present day. It has been reported that Japanese government researchers found that about 40% of the world's successful inventions in the last 70 years have come from Britain. By comparison, 25% came from the United States and 10% from Japan.

In order of their inventions, four British people whose inventions have made an important impact in recent years are:
- John Shepherd-Barron, who invented the ATM cash machine;
- Sir Tim Berners-Lee, who invented the World Wide Web, enabling us all to use the internet;
- Trevor Bayliss, who invented an eco-friendly radio, powered with a wind up handle. It allows people without electricity or batteries in poor parts of Africa to get information;
- Sir James Dyson, who invented the Dual Cyclone vacuum cleaner with no bag and the Air Multiplier, the fan with no blades.

NOTES
[1] Japan is sixth. According to the H-index. See http://www.scimagojr.com/countryrank.php

An early model of Dyson's Air Multiplier, a fan without blades.

Reading Comprehension

1. Which statement is true?
   a. Britain produces more scientific output than any other industrialized country.

Chapter 9 Science, inventions and business

b. Britain has won the second highest number of Nobel Prizes in science.
c. Britain has produced twice the number of successful modern inventions as America.

2. The people who should be most thankful to Tim Berners-Lee are people
   a. who use the internet.
   b. in poor African villages.
   c. who need to get money when the bank is closed.

This sign marks the spot of the first ATM at a bank just north of London.

Part 2 "Failures are finger posts on the road to achievement."

C. S. Lewis[2], the Oxford professor and children's writer, said the quote above. It's a positive way of thinking about failure. Inventors have many failures on the road to success. Both Bayliss and Dyson struggled for years before making the right invention and then getting funding to make their successful products. Other people never find success. One example was Arthur Pedrick, from southern England, who patented 162 inventions in the 1960s and 70s: *none* of them was made by a company. Two of his greatest ideas were a bicycle that could be ridden under water and "an arrangement whereby a car may be driven from the back seat."

That quotation comes from a funny book called *The Book of Heroic Failures*.[3] The book was very successful. Not all the failures described were British, but the British don't like people to take themselves too seriously. They enjoy stories of people who try hard, but fail. Another failure described in the book involved the *Royal Society for the Preventing of Accidents* (RoSPA), which promotes health and safety in England. Some years ago RoSPA tried to hold an event, but it was a complete failure because the whole display fell down.

NOTES
[2] C. S. Lewis is most famous for writing *The Chronicles of Narnia*. See chapter 13, p. 76.
[3] Written by Stephen Pile.

Reading Comprehension

3. Which statement is true?
   a. All British inventors fail first, and then succeed.
   b. Most British people consider inventors silly.
   c. Most British people find stories of failure funny.

Richard Arkwright built cotton mills (factories) in Derbyshire in the 18th century. Now it's a World Heritage site.

Welcome to Britain

Part 3 — R&D and manufacturing

Unfortunately for Britain, in contrast to the impressive records for science and inventions, the story of research and development (R & D) and manufacturing has been less good. According to the OECD[4], Britain's spending on R & D is much less than the G7 average, whereas Japan's is well above the average. Private British companies are more stingy than Japanese companies in contributing to their country's R & D budget.

The UK is the 6th biggest economy in the world according to its GDP.[5] Manufacturing has been steadily decreasing and has dropped to less than 20% of the economy. Over 80% now comes from providing services—in finance, IT, management consulting, law, architecture, the entertainment industry, and others[6]. Although many people have been relaxed about Britain being a leading post-industrial nation, others are concerned that the economy is not effectively balanced. They say Britain needs to make more things. Another concern is that over a quarter of what is made in Britain comes out of factories owned by foreign companies, especially American and German, but also Japanese, such as Toyota, Nissan and Honda.

Thousands of British manufacturing jobs have been lost due to the cost of production, and openness to foreign competition. The inventor James Dyson became successful enough to start his own company to make his products. But although Dyson kept the R & D section in southern England, he moved his factory to Malaysia to make the products more cheaply. Another recent example of lost jobs was when two companies bid for the contract to make trains. The British government awarded the big contract not to the English engineering firm (which had been making trains at Derby in the east midlands since 1839), but to a German company. Even the government's own Business Secretary said he was shocked. ∎

NOTES

[4] The Organisation for Economic Cooperation and Development.
[5] GDP = Gross Domestic Product (GDP), a way of measuring the size of a country's economy. The UK is behind Germany, Japan, China, and the USA.
[6] The remaining 0.6% comes from agriculture, which has become steadily smaller.

*R*eading *C*omprehension

4. Japan's companies
   a. spend less than Britain's companies on R & D.
   b. spend more than Britain's companies on R & D.
   c. make up 25% of Britain's manufacturing output.

5. Where are Dyson's bladeless Air Multipliers made?
   a. Southern England.
   b. Germany.
   c. Malaysia.

Structure Practice

a. Choose the one underlined word or phrase that should be corrected or rewritten. Then change it.

1. One of <u>the most</u> important 20th century <u>discovery</u> for the health of people <u>was</u> the antibiotic penicillin, <u>made by</u> the Scottish scientist, Alexander Fleming.

2. Britain's traditional <u>strong</u> in science is partly <u>a result of</u> having the world's <u>oldest</u> science association, the Royal Society, <u>which is</u> 350 years old.

b. Choose the one word or phrase that best completes the sentence.

3. .... Britain is a place of good ideas dependent on individuals, often without support from British industry in general, many Japanese companies have established R & D centres there.

   a. Noticeable   b. Notice   c. Noticed   d. Noticing

4. James Dyson's first international .... with his bagless vacuum cleaner was in Japan in 1991, when he won the International Design Fair prize.

   a. succeed   b. success   c. successful   d. successfully

5. The world's first modern railway line opened in 1830, ... Manchester and Liverpool in north west England.

   a. link   b. linking
   c. linked   d. linkage

Stephenson's *Rocket*, built in 1829 for the first railway between Manchester and Liverpool. Now it's in the Science Museum in London.

Welcome to Britain

Listening Challenge

Listen and fill in the missing words.

1. .... the OECD, the UK "shows a high degree of ...." in conducting original ....

2. The UK is one of the world's most globalized economies, ... , while British firms invest a lot in other countries.

3. The .... in recent years of a British company by a Japanese one was when .... company ARM, based in Cambridge.

4. Another ....-.................. purchase was the *Nikkei* Media Group .... influential *Financial Times* ...., based in London.

5. The biggest .... in the UK is Fujitsu, which employs 12,000 .... and .... for the ....

Going Further (for discussion or research)

1. From the information in this chapter, or your own research, what do you think is the most useful British invention? Why do you think so?

   ....

2. Choose two more British inventions with reasons, that have made the world better:

   ....

3. What do you think of C.S. Lewis' comment about failure?

   ....

Chapter 10

Politics and government

The Houses of Parliament with the leaning tower of Big Ben on the right. Left, on the south side of the River Thames, is the London Eye, built for the millennium celebrations in 2000. It's a big tourist attraction.

Vocabulary Focus

Match the words in the table with their definition below. Write the word on the line.

appoint	illegal
blow up	monarch
head of state	symbolic

symbolic   1. representing something, being a symbol

_____ 2. the leader of a country—e.g., president, king, queen, emperor, empress

_____ 3. to destroy something with an explosion

_____ 4. formally choose (someone for a position)

_____ 5. something not allowed in law, not legal

_____ 6. a ruler of a country by birth, e.g., a king or queen, emperor or empress

Part 1 Background

Like Japan, Britain has a Prime Minister (PM) as head of government, with two Houses of Parliament and a monarch as the symbolic head of state. However, there are two important differences. First, the representatives of Britain's upper house, the House of Lords, aren't elected; most are appointed by the government, some come from families from the aristocracy[1] and some are senior people in the Church of England. The role of the Lords is only to advise and examine proposals from the elected lower house, the House of Commons[2], of which the PM is a member. Some people say it would be more democratic if the Lords were elected, like Japan's House of Councillors[3]. But others argue it would be bad to let the upper house challenge the rights and power of the Commons.

The second important difference is that the monarch plays a more active role than in Japan. She meets the prime minister once a week to discuss the state of the country. PMs come and go with elections, but the monarch is there for life. Once a year the monarch officially opens parliament. For historical reasons, she's not allowed in the Commons so she enters the House of Lords and reads out to members of both houses the plans of the government in a speech written by the PM.

NOTES
[1] aristocracy = families of a high social rank with titles, the upper class「上流階級」.
[2] The House of Commons = Japan's House of Representatives, or「衆議院」.
[3]「参議院」

*R*eading *C*omprehension

1. In the British government system, which has the most power?
   a. The monarch, who is head of state.
   b. The House of Lords, which is unelected.
   c. The House of Commons, which is elected.

2. How is the British system different from Japanese one?
   a. The prime minister is a member of the lower house.
   b. The head of the royal family plays a more active role.
   c. The lower house has more power than the upper house.

The Prime Minister and other MPs debate in the House of Commons chamber.

Chapter 10 Politics and government

Part 2   Britain's leaders: human in good and bad ways

Although most Prime Ministers are graduates of Oxford University, they have recently seemed more like 'normal' people than PMs used to be. Three recent Prime Ministers had young families while living at the leader's official home in Downing Street, London. The wives of two, Tony Blair and David Cameron, even gave birth while their husbands were leading the country. In addition, the British are also familiar with having a female Prime Minister. Margaret Thatcher was the first. The second was Theresa May, who became PM in 2016 after Cameron resigned, following his failure in the EU referendum. Interestingly, both female PMs were leader of the Conservative Party, which has many fewer female MPs than its rival Labour.

Armed police guard the gates of London's Downing Street where the Prime Minister lives.

It is also true, though, that various scandals, questionable decisions such as joining the Iraq War in 2003, and bad behavior by politicians, the police, and the media have lost a lot of people's trust in recent years. People are much less respectful of their leaders than before.

*R*eading *C*omprehension

3. Why do British people trust their leaders less than before?
   a. Because there have been two female Prime Ministers.
   b. Because some prime ministers have had babies while in office.
   c. Because of various scandals involving people in important institutions.

Part 3   Would you like to join a party?

The British parliament is often called a two party system because the government has either been from the Conservative Party or the Labour Party. The former is more right-wing and traditionally the party of business, while the latter is more left-wing and started—as its name shows—to represent ordinary workers. In recent years their policy differences have been less clear. The coalition government of 2010–15 was made by the Conservatives joining with the Liberal Democrats, a smaller, economically right-wing, socially left-wing, party.

These days, the differences in support are clearer by region. Most of the Liberal Democratic support is in western England. Labour is strong in towns and cities throughout Britain. The Conservatives are strong in the countryside and suburbs, especially in southern England. In Scotland the strongest party is the Scottish National Party which wants full independence from England. The SNP is now the biggest party in the Scottish parliament.

In Wales the main parties are Labour, Plaid Cymru (which means the Party of Wales and wants independence for Wales), and the Conservatives. In Northern Ireland there is a mix of nationalist parties and others with links to the main parties in Britain. ■

Why did a man called Guy Fawkes try to blow up the Houses of Parliament?

When the British strongly doubt the honesty of their representatives in parliament they sometimes joke that the only person who entered the building with an honest intention was Guy Fawkes. That's because he tried to blow it up! In 1605 Fawkes and some friends planned to blow up the Houses of Parliament and kill King James I* when he was visiting to open the new session. Fawkes was angry with new laws against Catholics; James was strongly Protestant. Fawkes was caught by soldiers under parliament and hanged. One of Britain's unique and important festivals celebrates his failure, on or around November 5th. It's known as Bonfire Day; in parks around the country there are fireworks events and bonfires on top of which models of Guy, made from old clothes, are burned.

NOTES

* James was Scottish and was also James VI of Scotland. He was invited to become James I of England after the death of Elizabeth I, because she left no heir, and he was—like her—Protestant.

Reading Comprehension

4. Which statement is NOT true?
   a. Labour gets most of its support from lower income people in cities and towns.
   b. The Scottish Nationalists are known as Plaid Cymru.
   c. The Liberal Democrats took part in a coalition government from 2010 to 2015.

5. Which statement is NOT true?
   a. Guy Fawkes was angry with anti-Catholic laws.
   b. Many fireworks events are held in November.
   c. Guy Fawkes blew up the Houses of Parliament.

Chapter 10   Politics and government

*S*tructure *P*ractice

a. Choose the one underlined word or phrase that should be corrected or rewritten. Then change it.

1. Britain <u>is</u> unusual in that it <u>doesn't</u> have one constitutional document <u>in the way</u> that, for example, Japan and the United States <u>does</u>.

2. Different parts of the constitution are written down in different documents and some parts of it aren't <u>wrote down</u> anywhere; these areas of government <u>are</u> somehow just <u>understood</u> from the way they <u>have developed</u> over time.

3. The first document which officially <u>tries to</u> limit the powers of the king was the Magna Carta in 1215. It <u>has influenced</u> the constitutions of other countries <u>as well as</u> the way Britain <u>is run</u>.

b. Choose the one word or phrase that best completes the sentence.

4. After the 2017 election, the Conservatives were still the biggest single party in Parliament, but needed {a/an} .... with a small, Protestant party in Northern Ireland to be able to stay in office.

   a. agreement   b. debate   c. decision   d. opportunity

5. The leaders of the Conservatives and Labour have a tough job to keep their parties together as they are both divided between moderates and members with more .... views.

   a. cautious   b. extreme   c. intelligent   d. stupid

*L*istening *C*hallenge

Listen and fill in the missing words.

1. In Britain .... when you become officially an .... at .... years old.

2. Until .... British people .... adult at the ....

3. Only .... British Prime Ministers out of the last 14 didn't .... either .... or .... University.

4. .... of those four Prime Ministers .... to university at all.

5. Recent .... show that Britain is increasingly divided by .... and the countryside, and by .... and ....

Going Further (for discussion or research)

1. Are you glad Japan has lowered the voting age to 18?

   ....

2. Some countries, such as Australia, make it illegal not to vote in elections because it makes people participate in politics. What do you think of that?

   ....

3. What do you think of Britain's system of an unelected, but weak House of Lords in contrast with Japan's elected, but more powerful House of Councillors?

   ....

The Houses of Parliament, officially called the Palace of Westminster.
Big Ben is the bell inside the clock tower on the right.

Chapter 11

Food

A village pub serving food as well as drinks on a summer's day.

Vocabulary Focus

Match the words in the table with their definition below. Write the word on the line.

disapproving	obesity
ingredients	recipe
invent	silly

disapproving 1. not approving, showing dislike

_____ 2. instructions that tell you how to cook something

_____ 3. parts of a food dish, e.g., an egg in an omelette

_____ 4. the condition of being extremely fat and very overweight

_____ 5. to make something new

_____ 6. not sensible, foolish

Part 1   Background

Can you guess what a *foodie* is? It doesn't mean someone who eats too much. Britain is second only to the United States as a country where the problem of obesity is threatening the health of the nation. Eating too much junk food (sugary and salty snacks, such as crisps[1], biscuits and chocolate) and high calorie fast food, such as Big Macs, is normal. No, *foodie* describes someone who takes a keen interest in food, in cooking, in the ingredients used to make various dishes, in recipes, in the preparation of food, in the art of presenting it, and in eating well[2]. Everyone has heard of the bad reputation of British food, but a *foodie* is someone with food for a hobby. Can foodies really exist in Britain?

The word foodie is significant for the following three reasons. First, it was invented only 30 years ago but is now frequently used, especially in the media. That means a reasonable number of people are showing such an interest in food. Second, it's often used with a rather disapproving tone, as if it's silly to be so interested in good food. Third, it's an informal word which ends in *-ie* so it sounds quite childish, as if it's not really an interest worthy of respect. The first significance is a sign that food is improving, but the second and third points warn us that taking care to cook and eat good food is not considered normal.

NOTES
[1] Crisps are potato chips in American English.
[2] The originally French word gourmet only really means the last of these, eating well.

(L), one of London's oldest pubs.
(R), fish and chips & mushy peas.

Reading Comprehension

1. Britain has a problem with
   a. too many people interested in food.
   b. too many overweight people.
   c. too many interesting recipes.

2. The appearance of foodies shows
   a. being especially interested in food is still not usual in Britain.
   b. the reputation of British food is wrong.
   c. most British people don't like eating.

Part 2 Convenience food

Convenience food: prepared meals, ready for heating up, and a wide choice of sandwiches (below).

The writer George Mikes, who became British after being brought up in Hungary, observed that in most European countries people had "good food; in England they have good table manners."[3] Many years later, he joked that the food had got better, but the table manners worse. The truth, as a more recent observer wrote, is that the food isn't so bad, but that it is "not given the same high priority in English life as it is elsewhere."[4] Although supermarkets offer plenty of fresh, good quality fruit and vegetables, meat and fish, a lot of British people rarely cook meals which require much effort. Instead, they live on convenience food.

Convenience meals are already prepared and cooked, and need only to be heated up in the microwave or oven for eating. Another type of convenience food is sandwiches, which are the most popular lunch food and available everywhere. They were invented in the 18th century by the Earl of Sandwich who didn't want to stop either his gambling or political work to eat a proper, cooked meal—a true Englishman!

NOTES
[3] This was published in 1946 in *How to be an alien*.
[4] Kate Fox, in *Watching the English*.

Reading Comprehension

3. Which statement is true?
    a. Convenience meals, including sandwiches, are very popular in Britain.
    b. Despite its bad reputation, food in Britain is given high priority.
    c. George Mikes was born in Hungary, but felt more hungry in Britain.

Part 3 Britain's favourite foods

The popularity of convenience food is only part of the picture, however. The food in pubs and restaurants throughout the country has greatly improved in recent years. The number of restaurants in the U.K. awarded at least one Michelin star has been increasing and in 2011 reached 140.

Somerset Maugham, 1874–1965

In London you can find cuisines from about 80 different countries. The first Indian restaurant opened in 1810. Now there are about 10,000 around the country. Curry is so popular it's not really 'foreign' any more. In fact, the curry *chicken tikka masala* was for several years Britain's most popular dish and a former Foreign Secretary[5] described it as a "true British national dish". And he was right because although *chicken tikka* came from India, the creamy sauce *masala* was invented by an Indian chef in Glasgow! But *masala* isn't really spicy and tastes change. Now British people like spicier curries and their new favourite is *jalfrezi*.

Where does this leave traditional British food? Many years ago, the English writer Somerset Maugham said, "If you want to eat well in England, you have to eat breakfast three times a day." That's because the *Full English* breakfast of eggs, bacon, sausage, tomatoes, baked beans, mushrooms, sometimes kipper (a smoked fish), followed by toast with marmalade, is a delicious and healthy way to start the day. But few people eat it at home now. They have cereals with milk and/or toast, washed down with tea or coffee. Like in Japan, yoghurt has become a choice for the health-conscious.

A cooked English breakfast

Only a few restaurants in Britain serve traditional British food, dishes such as roast beef or lamb or *game*[6], or steak and kidney pie, with potatoes and vegetables. But one traditional fast food remains popular—fish and chips. Another dish which has become popular outside Britain is the Cornish pasty, a baked pastry filled with beef, potato and other vegetables, originally from Devon and Cornwall, in western England. One food which has *not* successfully travelled the world is Marmite. Loved by many people in Britain but hated by others, it's a salty, yeast-based spread for bread. It is high in vitamin B and goes well with cheese but it has a strong taste and smell. Be warned! ∎

NOTES
[5] The Foreign Secretary is the government's chief foreign minister.
[6] Game is birds and animals hunted for food, such as deer, pheasant, goose, rabbit etc.

Marmite (with bread and cheese)

Reading Comprehension

4. Britain's most popular dish for many years was invented in
   a. London.
   b. India and Scotland.
   c. Devon in western England.

5. Which statement is true?
   a. To eat well, English people used to eat breakfast three times a day.
   b. People have strong feelings about Marmite.
   c. Fish and chips isn't popular any more.

Structure Practice

a. Choose the one underlined word or phrase that should be corrected or rewritten. Then change it.

1. Friendly women used to present most cooking programmes on television but most cooking stars now are more aggressive, male celebrity chefs who appear on TV as well as managing restaurants in Britain and around the world.

2. One of the celebrity chef, Jamie Oliver, ran a campaign to improve the quality of food served in schools.

b. Choose the one word or phrase that best completes the sentence.

3. Pizza and pasta, ... Italian of course, are very popular, and even Japanese sushi and noodles are increasingly available.

    a. origin		b. originality		c. original		d. originally

4. .... 1997, the amount of convenience food eaten in Britain has increased by 300 per cent.

    a. After		b. From		c. In		d. Since

5. Working class people usually call lunch 'dinner' and their evening meal 'tea'; the upper and upper-middle classes call their evening .... 'supper' unless it's a more formal event in which case they say 'dinner'.

    a. dinner		b. lunch		c. meal		d. snack

Welcome to Britain

Listening Challenge

Listen and fill in the missing words.

1. One sign of more .... being shown by British people at .... is the return in .... of porridge oats, eaten the Scottish way with .... and a pinch of ....

2. If you want to eat .... the traditional way, you should .... them with .... and ....

3. The first .... restaurant in Britain opened just over .... years ago; now there are .... thousand proper restaurants and .... thousand takeaways, or carry-outs![7]

4. Puddings, also known as ...., ..., or afters, such as .... pie or ...., are a popular part of British meals.

5. .... class people always call any dessert which is not fruit '...............'; dessert is a .... word.

NOTES

[7] A 'takeaway' is what American English calls a takeout. Scottish people say 'carry out'. It can be a kind of restaurant, or a whole meal which the customer takes away to eat.

A traditional dessert in a modern style: bread and butter pudding with ice-cream.

Going Further (for discussion or research)

1. What do you think of British food?

   ....

2. What British food would you like to try?

   ....

3. If you were allowed to eat only one more meal ever, but you had a free choice of food, what dish would you choose?

   ....

Chapter 12

Music and fashion

Singer-songwriter Amy Winehouse, 1983–2011.

Vocabulary Focus

Match the words in the table with their definition below. Write the word on the line.

aggressive	ponytail
eagerly	rivalry
invasion	swear

eagerly   1. wanting something very much

_____ 2. a hairstyle in which the person's hair is tied up at the back and hangs down like a tail

_____ 3. use bad or offensive language

_____ 4. ready to attack

_____ 5. conflict or competition between people in the same area

_____ 6. a large number of people entering another, often foreign, place

Welcome to Britain

Part 1 Background

Although rock and roll and the modern pop industry started in America in the mid-1950s, it was soon eagerly followed by the working class youth of Britain. Most young people left school at 15 and got jobs in the booming economy so they had money to spend, along with more freedom and leisure time to enjoy themselves. By the mid-1960s the Americans were referring to 'the British invasion', as the Beatles and then others, such as the Rolling Stones, sold records, toured and wowed audiences in the United States. Since that time the British along with the Americans have led the pop music world.

The faces of the Beatles.

Even from its early days, pop music has gone hand in hand with fashion. Pop musicians and fashion designers, such as Mary Quant and Vivienne Westwood, have influenced each other and made important contributions to British culture and to the country's economy.

Britain's first clear group of teenagers, its first youth subculture, appeared in the 1950s. Their music was British skiffle (very basic rock n roll) and then American rock n roll. They were called *teddy boys*, or *teds*, because their clothes were modelled on the dandies of Edwardian Britain[1] forty years before. Teddy is a short form of the name Edward. They dressed in long jackets with velvet collars, narrow 'drainpipe' trousers worn short to show their socks. They wore their hair long, but brushed back and held in place with oil. *Teddy girls* wore pencil skirts and did their hair in ponytails.

A pencil skirt

NOTES

[1] This refers to the years 1901–10, when the king was Edward VII.

Reading Comprehension

1. What was the 1960s 'British invasion'?
   a. The British army during the American War of Independence.
   b. American rock and roll becoming popular in Britain.
   c. British pop groups becoming popular in the U.S.A.

2. Which statement is NOT true?
   a. The name Edward is sometimes shortened to Teddy.
   b. Teddy boys and teddy girls liked rock and roll music.
   c. Britain's first teenage subculture appeared in the Edwardian era.

Teddy boys

Chapter 12   Music and fashion

Part 2   Women rule in the early 21st century

In recent years there has been a more 'anything goes' feel to fashion. The most successful young British male pop artist has been Ed Sheeran, but many others have been female. Examples include Dido, Lily Allen (who got noticed through the internet site Myspace), and Adele, whose second and third albums stayed for several weeks at number one in the U.S. and many other countries.

Probably the most talented of all was the daughter of a London taxi driver, Amy Winehouse, whose album *Back to Black* was considered one of the best in the early 21st century. She also looked great in photographs with her unique style. It influenced the American pop and fashion icon Lady Gaga. But like many in the rock business before, Winehouse consumed too many drugs and too much alcohol and died, aged 27, in 2011.

*R*eading *C*omprehension

3. Which statement is NOT true?
   a. In recent years there hasn't been one strong fashion style.
   b. The only successful British pop artists recently have been women.
   c. Amy Winehouse made a strong impression with her music and fashion.

Part 3   Pop subcultures come and go

The British media likes reporting conflict, and when reporting on youth subcultures in the past, it has often focused on rivalry between gangs. In the early-mid-1960s the rivals were the *mods* and the *rockers*. The rockers wore leather jackets, rode big motorbikes and liked rock n roll. The mods, short for *modernists*, dressed stylishly in Italian style suits, slip-on shoes and parkers. They rode Italian scooters and danced to urban black American soul music, as well as Jamaican ska and the English bands *The Who*, the *Small Faces*, and *The Kinks*. As the 1960s music developed, so did the fashions. Mary Quant introduced the mini-skirt in 1964.

The next rivalry was between *hippies* and *skinheads*. Hippy styles, based on loose, flowery-patterned clothes went with more experimental drug-influenced music. The song which simply expressed their ideas at that time was *All You Need*

Is Love by The Beatles.

The skinheads were aggressive-looking, dressed in jeans cut short and high boots along with tight fitting shirts and hair shaved very short. In their early days they grew out of the fashions of the mods and Jamaican *rude boys*, who had come to live in England in the late 1950s. Their music, too, was similar at that time to what the mods had liked.

The 1970s were the era first of *glam*² *rock* and then punk. Punk's songs were short, and played fast and loud. The most famous group was *The Sex Pistols*. They were banned from television after swearing on a live show. The most famous designer was Vivienne Westwood. Features of punk fashion included ripped jeans, lots of zippers and pins, lots of PVC and Mohican style hair cuts.

The fashion subculture of the 1980s, which grew out of glam rock, was the New Romantic. It was connected with electronic pop. One of the best bands was called *Japan*.

In the 1990s guitar bands like *Oasis* and *Blur* openly admired the famous bands of the 1960s. Britpop and another sort of mod revival with union jacks on clothes were in fashion for a few years. But bands come and go, fashions change and Britpop was soon over. ∎

NOTES
² Glam is short for glamour.

*R*eading *C*omprehension

4. Which pair were NOT rivals?
   a. Britpop and New Romantic.
   b. Hippies and skinheads.
   c. Mods and rockers.

5. Which music and fashion group is Vivienne Westwood closely identified with?
   a. Mods.
   b. Punk.
   c. Glam rock.

The most famous punk singer: Johnny Rotten of the Sex Pistols.

Chapter 12 Music and fashion

Structure Practice

a. Choose the one word or phrase that best completes the sentence.

1. Between about 1960 and 1990 there was a big .... gap between the dress styles of the young and the middle aged. Before that time even the young dressed in a middle-aged way; now middle-aged people often dress in a young way.

   a. clothes   b. education   c. generation   d. musical

2. Most people used to hear new songs on the radio before .... the latest records.

   a. buy   b. buying   c. bought   d. breaking

3. It's more usual now for people to discover singers and bands on You Tube and internet social network sites and to care .... if they're new or old.

   a. for   b. little   c. much   d. mainly

b. Choose the one word or phrase that should be corrected. Then correct it.

4. Nowadays young <u>person</u> seem to have less prejudice <u>against</u> the pop music of <u>a few</u> years before than they <u>used to</u>.

5. Even the Beatles, who <u>stopped records</u> before more than half of the world's population <u>was born</u>, are popular again in Britain; having <u>broken up</u> in 1970, 30 years ago they were <u>more popular</u> in Japan.

Listening Challenge

Listen and fill in the missing words.

1. In the .... , Britain's .... was known as .... , and Carnaby Street was the height of ....

2. The time of the .... and .... was memorably .... *Quadrophenia*.

3. The .... by the band Japan, who once played with Ryuichi Sakamoto, was on 16 .... in ....

4. Susan Boyle, from .... , ... on NHK's .........-......-...............
   year end song show, but while some people .... ,
   no one has followed her ....

5. Pop music and fashion have often ....

Going Further (for discussion or research)

1. Which British bands or singers do you like?

   ....

2. Have you ever sung a song in English? Which one? Where did you sing it?

   ....

3. Which pop fashions do you like?

   ....

4. Which pop fashions don't you like?

   ....

One of London's most famous pop bands from the 1960s are The Kinks. A pub, near where they grew up, is dedicated to the band, led by brothers Ray and Dave Davies. One of their songs is called, *Dedicated Follower of Fashion*.

Chapter 13

Fantasy and castles

The Mad Hatter's Tea Party in *Alice in Wonderland*.

Vocabulary Focus

Match the words in the table with their definition below. Write the word on the line.

influential	selfish
nominate	substantial
remains	visually

__remains__   1. parts of something left after most has been destroyed

_____   2. formally suggest or propose

_____   3. having a lot of influence

_____   4. in a way to be seen, such as with pictures or film

_____   5. thinking only of himself or herself, not about others

_____   6. a large amount

73

Part 1 Background

For some people, Britain is a land of fantasy and castles. Fantasy is a genre of literature which has grown in popularity since the 19th century. Fantasy is often considered mainly children's literature, probably as a result of *Alice's Adventures in Wonderland* by Lewis Carroll. One of the earliest, famous and influential examples in the modern history of fantasy, it was published in 1865.

The castles are much older. Most were built in the 500 years following 1066. That was the year William of Normandy, in northern France, attacked England and defeated the English king in battle. Castles had been built since the century before in France. In order to show his power and keep his position as King of England, William then built them all over England and Wales. Later, castles were built in Scotland and Ireland, too. For a long time they played important military, economic and social roles. Castles no longer play a military role and thousands have now disappeared. But there are still several hundred castles in the UK with substantial remains. Most still have an economic role, attracting large numbers of tourists. Many still play a social role: some castles are homes and an increasing number are popular locations for weddings. It has become quite fashionable in recent years for people to get married in a castle.

The remains of Dunstanburgh Castle in Northumberland, north east England.

Reading Comprehension

1. Which statement is NOT true?
    a. Castles were built in France before they were built in England.
    b. The modern genre of fantasy literature started in the 19th century.
    c. The author of *Alice in Wonderland* was William of Normandy.

2. What are castles used for now?
    a. Living in, tourism, and weddings.
    b. Living in and for housing soldiers in training.
    c. Protecting England from attacks by French soldiers.

Part 2   Britain and Japan linked in fantasy

A few years ago the Japanese film animation director Hayao Miyazaki was nominated for an Academy Award for his *Howl's Moving Castle*. The story was based on the novel by the English fantasy writer for children, Diana Wynne Jones. Both in English and Japanese, her stories were perfect for the anime talents of Mr Miyazaki and Studio Ghibli to bring them to life visually. Long before, in 1983–84 NHK showed an anime series called *Fushigi no Kuni no Arisu*, based on the *Alice in Wonderland* story. And of course more recently the Harry Potter series sold millions of books and won thousands of fans in Japan, not just thanks to the author J. K. Rowling, but also to the Japanese translator, Yuko Matsuoka. Although Rowling says there won't be any more books, she has established the Pottermore website, so people can keep in touch with Harry and Hermione and the others.

The dining hall of Christchurch College, Oxford, where parts of the Harry Potter movies were filmed.

Countries can influence each other in their popular culture and recently the popularity of anime and manga characters has spread from Japan to Britain. There's now a big, annual event in London called Hyper Japan, which features anime and Cosplay fans dressed in the costumes of their favourite characters.

Reading Comprehension

3. The two names associated with *Howl's Moving Castle* are
   a. J.K. Rowling and Yuko Matsuoka.
   b. Diana Wynne Jones and Hyper Japan.
   c. Diana Wynne Jones and Hayao Miyazaki.

Part 3   Fantasy and films

Fantasy stories are attractive to imaginative film makers. The Harry Potter novels have made the most successful film series, while many other fantasy novels have also been filmed, some of them many times. For example, about 20 films based

It is popular for Harry Potter fans to pose for a photo at the Hogwarts train platform at Kings Cross station in London.

on *Alice in Wonderland* have been made since the beginning of the 19-hundreds. Another popular story for movie makers has been *Peter Pan*, about the young boy who can fly and doesn't grow up. Hollywood sometimes changes things from the original, though. In the original theatre play and novel, Peter Pan is rather a selfish and childish boy, whereas in the Walt Disney animation he's quite brave.

One reason for the great interest in fantasy stories in recent years is the Harry Potter novels and films. Another reason is that the power of computer-generated special effects has made it easier to bring fantasy stories excitingly to the big screen. Recent examples have been *Lord of the Rings* (filmed in three parts), *The Chronicles of Narnia*, and *The Golden Compass*. The first was written by J. R. R. Tolkien, who also wrote *The Hobbit*. Tolkien was born in South Africa but became a professor of English at Oxford University. His close friend C.S. Lewis, also an Oxford professor but born in Northern Ireland, wrote the Narnia stories. Another writer who taught at Oxford is Philip Pullman. He wrote a series of three stories called *His Dark Materials*. The first, *Northern Lights*, was made into the film called *The Golden Compass*.

A few years ago, the BBC ran a competition to find 'the nation's best-loved book'. Over six months, 750,000 people voted, and the winner was Tolkien's *Lord of the Rings*. Three other fantasy stories, including *His Dark Materials* and *Harry Potter*, came in the top five. ∎

Reading Comprehension

4. Which note about the films is NOT correct?
   a. Harry Potter—a successful series.
   b. Lord of the Rings—a trilogy.
   c. Northern Lights—from the story by Philip Pullman.

5. Apart from writing fantasy stories, what links Tolkien, Lewis and Pullman?
   a. They were all born outside England.
   b. They all taught at Oxford University.
   c. They all wrote stories in three parts.

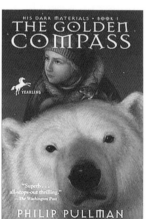

Chapter 13 Fantasy and castles

Structure Practice

a. Choose the one underlined word or phrase that should be corrected or rewritten. Then change it.

1. According to Wikipedia, the remains of 800 castles are still visible in England and Wales and "300 castles have substantial survival stone or brick remains".

2. Lewis Carroll's real name was Charles Dodgson. He wrote down *Alice in Wonderland* after made the story up to entertain the children of a friend of his during a boat trip.

b. Choose the one word or phrase that best completes the sentence.

3. Harry Potter is a teenage ……………… .

   a. lizard   b. philosopher   c. witch   d. wizard

4. There were seven Harry Potter novels but eight films, as the story of the last book was ……………… into two films.

   a. spilled   b. split   c. mixed   d. told

5. Recent Japanese guest stars that ……………… at Hyper Japan* include the cello-playing Japanese singer Kanon Wakeshima.

   a. appear   b. appearing   c. have appeared   d. had appeared

   NOTES
   *For the most recent information on Hyper Japan, see <https://hyperjapan.co.uk>

Listening Challenge

Listen and fill in the missing words.

1. The famous Tower of London ……… ………… by Londoners when the ……… ……… from France, William the Conqueror, built it in the 11th century to ……… ………… ………… .

2. But now the Tower is enjoyed ……… …… …………… of England's long history and as good for …… ……… ……………… , attracting over ……… million visitors a year.

77

3. Many .... across the UK are now open as ....

4. The Eagle and .... pub in Oxford is famous as the place where C. S. Lewis, J. R. R. Tolkien and others met every .... for many years to .... and ....[1]

5. The .... *Neverland*, starring Johnny Depp, is about J.M. Barrie, the author of Peter Pan, ... being the name of the .... where .... and Tinker Bell lived.

NOTES
[1] The group were called the Inklings (because they were writers who used ink).

The statue of Peter Pan in Kensington Gardens, London

Going Further (for discussion or research)

1. Which fantasy stories have you read?

   ....

2. Which fantasy films have you seen?

   ....

3. Which is your favourite fantasy story?

   ....

4. Would you like to stay, or get married, in a castle?

   ....

The entrance to a children's theatrical show about Alice in Wonderland. It was shown in some old tunnels in London.

Chapter 14

Language

William Shakespeare, England's national poet and playwright, 1564–1616.

Vocabulary Focus

Match the words in the table with their definition below. Write the word on the line.

crossword	posh
dialect	rhyme
intellectual	sensationalism

__intellectual__ 1. a person who spends a lot of time thinking about difficult ideas

_____ 2. a word game in which you work out answers from clues and write the words in square boxes

_____ 3. a way of presenting stories or facts to make people feel excited or angry

_____ 4. a form of language spoken in a particular area

_____ 5. use words which end in the same *sound*, e.g., me / sea

_____ 6. fancy, connected to the upper class

Part 1 Background

Like Japanese, the English language has developed through several stages into the language we know today. There are three main periods: Old English, from about the year 450 to 1100; Middle English, from around 1100 to 1500, and the Modern English period since.

Britain's most famous writer, Shakespeare, was writing and performing his plays just before and after 1600. Many changes were occurring then and have since, so we cannot be sure how his plays sounded. We do know Shakespeare used various spellings for words and even spelled his own name in different ways! One thing experts have worked out is that Shakespeare added about 1,700 words or phrases to the language. Examples include: bloody, generous, hurry, lonely, obscene, suspicious.

Winston Churchill, 1874–1965.

Literature has always been regarded highly in British culture. Writers are more famous than other kinds of artists. The love of words reaches all parts of society. Winston Churchill, Prime Minister during the Second World War, was famous for his speeches and won the Nobel Prize for Literature. Much English humour is based on word play, not just by professional writers and comedians, but also by ordinary people making puns[1] in daily life. All daily newspapers, from the quality papers read by educated intellectuals, to the sensationalist tabloids read by people with only basic education, contain one or two crosswords *every day*. For some readers the crosswords are more important than all the articles.

NOTES
[1] pun「洒落、言葉遊び」

Reading Comprehension

1. The works of William Shakespeare come from the time of
   a. Old English.
   b. Middle English.
   c. Early Modern English.

2. Which statement is true?
   a. Winston Churchill won the Nobel Peace Prize.
   b. All kinds of British people enjoy doing crosswords.
   c. Only educated intellectuals in Britain enjoy playing with words.

Part 2 Language and social class

The Irish playwright George Bernard Shaw famously wrote, "It is impossible for an Englishman to open his mouth without making some other Englishman hate or despise[2] him." This was about 100 years ago, but even today people are often judged on how they speak. If their regional accent is too strong they may be looked down on as lower class. But if they sound like a member of the royal family or someone from the upper or upper-middle classes, they may be hated for being 'posh'. A lot of people, therefore, now speak something called Estuary English, which is based on the London accent but is rather classless.

The connection between class and language involves vocabulary too. Upper and upper-middle class people look down on those who say 'Pardon?' because it's short for "I beg your pardon." This sounds too polite for people who don't need to care what others think. The upper class say, "What?" or, when being more polite, "Sorry? What?" The middle and lower middle-classes use "Pardon?" because they think "What?" sounds rude; also, too 'common'—because "Wha(t)?", often with the 't' almost silent in a glottal stop[3], is the word used mostly by the lower classes!

NOTES
[2] despise = to have a low opinion of someone or something
[3] glottal stop「声門閉鎖音」

*R*eading *C*omprehension

3. Which statement is NOT true?
   a. English people's way of speaking and vocabulary can show their social class.
   b. Some English people have a prejudice against the way other English people speak.
   c. "Pardon?" is the upper class way to mean, "Could you say that again, please?"

Dr Johnson's House in London. Samuel Johnson, 1709–84, was a writer. His most impressive achievement was making the first dictionary of the English language. It was published in 1755 after 9 years work.

Part 3 Rhyming slang and American English

Cockney rhyming slang is one example of a dialect developed by members of a class—the working class of the east end of London. They invented new phrases to communicate in a way that couldn't be understood by others, in particular the police. A famous example is *apples and pears* to mean *stairs*, as pears rhymes with stairs. But that phrase is rarely used now.

Two examples which *are* used in daily life by many people—not only Cockneys—are "Use your loaf!" to mean "Think!" and "Let's have a butcher's" to mean, "Let me have a look." How do these phrases work? Well, they're interesting because the rhyming words have been dropped. The first comes from *loaf of bread*; *bread* rhymes with *head* and if you 'use your head' you think. The second comes *from butcher's hook* which is used to hang meat; *hook* rhymes with *look*.

The number of British people speaking English is now millions fewer than the numbers of Americans and speakers of other first languages who communicate with each other in English. Most people now accept that the English don't 'own' the language. But some people are annoyed with the increasing use of American English even in Britain, such as *train station* for *railway station*, *truck* instead of *lorry* and *movie* being used more than *film*. The British English word *wireless* has been replaced by the originally American *radio*, but some people still say *telly* for TV.

It's interesting that some words for new technology have developed differently: *cell* phone in America but *mobile* phone in Britain; *ATM* in America but *cash machine* in Britain. *Smartphone*, however, is the same on both sides of the Atlantic.

British spellings, such as organisation, traveller and colour, are still used and British people still say "he's in hospital", not "he's in the hospital" which Americans say. Pronunciation, not just accent, can be different. For example, while Americans say secretary in 4 syllables, the British use only 3: /sekrətri/. ∎

*R*eading *C*omprehension

4. Which statement is true?
   a. Rhyming slang is rarely used now.
   b. Rhyming slang was originally used by the police.
   c. Rhyming slang has been adapted into daily life by many people.

5. Which three language items are all British English?
   a. In the hospital, traveler, ATM.
   b. In hospital, labour, cash machine.
   c. Wireless, organize, train station.

A travelling library in Suffolk, eastern England. The bus, full of books for borrowing, moves around small towns and villages without a library of their own.

*S*tructure *P*ractice

a. Choose the one underlined word or phrase that should be corrected or rewritten. Then change it.

1. <u>During</u> the Middle English period there were many changes <u>in</u> the language, starting <u>with</u> French words (such as *government* and *pork*) brought into English <u>for</u> a consequence of the Norman Conquest in 1066.

2. In that year the English king was <u>died</u> in battle and <u>replaced</u> as ruler by William of Normandy, in northern France. For the next 200 years French <u>was</u> the language of the ruling class in England, but the majority of the people always <u>spoke</u> English.

b. Choose the one word or phrase that best completes the sentence.

3. Before they .... married in 2011, Prince William and Kate Middleton broke up for a few months, partly, it was said, because she was only middle-class.

   a. get   b. got   c. getting   d. gotten

4. It was reported that members of the royal family objected to Kate's mother because she said, "..............." during a visit to the Queen's holiday castle in Scotland.

   a. Eh?   b. Repeat, please.   c. Pardon?   d. What?

5. The comic operas of Gilbert and Sullivan, still performed today over a hundred years after their deaths, are enjoyed more for the clever and funny lyrics of Gilbert rather than .... for the music of Sullivan.

   a. admiration   b. admire   c. admired   d. admiringly

Welcome to Britain

Listening Challenge

Listen and fill in the missing words.

1. It's been said that Britain and America are ....
by a ....

2. Some British people don't like 'Americanisms' such as *gotten* as the past participle of *get*—but .... and gradually .... from .... English.

3. One reason English has such a .... is that .... freely use .... , such as tsunami, from other languages.*

4. Some middle-class .... and comedians speak publicly in a working-class or Estuary English .... because they fear they will be .... if they sound posh.

5. If you want someone to think about a problem, you can say, ".................. ...."

Going Further (for discussion or research)

1. What's your favourite English word?

    ....

2. Do you prefer the sound of British English or American English? Why?

    ....

3. What do you think of rhyming slang?

    ....

4. Another example of rhyming slang is *dog and bone* for *phone*. Try to invent your own rhyming slang phrase for something:

    ....

NOTES
* This is like Japanese, but in contrast with French which has an academy which tries to decide which foreign words will be allowed and which are forbidden.

Chapter 15

The arts

London's West End has many theatres showing plays and musicals, starring famous actors.

Vocabulary Focus

Match the words in the table with their definition below. Write the word on the line.

literary	second-hand
passionate	verbal
poet	visual

__*poet*__ 1. someone who writes poetry

_____ 2. expressed in pictures or by something you can see

_____ 3. very strong feelings or a strong belief

_____ 4. already used, not new

_____ 5. expressed in speech or with words

_____ 6. connected with literature

Part 1 Background

It's sometimes been said that Britain is more of a verbal culture than a visual one. There are signs this is changing with new art galleries opening, and outside art works on display, in various parts of the country. Younger artists like Tracey Emin and Damien Hirst, too, have caught the public's imagination. But, as we read in the chapter on Language, British people like words. The average person would find it easier to name a famous British writer than a famous British painter or classical musician. There has even been a renewed interest in poetry, especially as some modern poets write in a more direct way that's easier for ordinary people to understand.

Shakespeare was a poet, but is more famous for his plays, of course. One of the few things that he would find familiar if he returned to London would be the strength of the theatre, about 400 years after his death. Both the Royal Shakespeare and the National Theatre companies (both supported by government money) and the private theatres continue to attract thousands of customers, even during bad economic times. London has about 120 theatres, but almost each town or city has at least one theatre featuring professional or skilled amateur actors. Some regional theatres, such as the Everyman in Liverpool, are famous for their excellent productions.

One of the most popular theatre genres in recent years has been the musical. This is the form of musical performance where words are as important as the music in telling the story. Nevertheless, one of Britain's richest men is Andrew Lloyd Webber, who has composed the music for many successful musicals, including *Cats* and the *Phantom of the Opera*. But classical opera, as well as classical music in general, also attracts passionate fans, and world famous singers, conductors and musicians perform at venues in London and elsewhere.

Reading Comprehension

1. Which statement is NOT true?
   a. Traditionally, British people are more comfortable with word-based artistic works than visual arts.
   b. The theatre was strong in Shakespeare's day and is still strong now.
   c. People stopped going to the theatre in the economic recession.

Chapter 15   The arts

2. Andrew Lloyd Webber has got rich by
    a. writing the words for some musicals.
    b. writing the music for some musicals.
    c. composing opera music.

The Minack Theatre, an open air theatre built next to the sea in Cornwall.

Part 2   Literary festivals

Poets, novelists and other writers don't just write books. They read their work aloud and take part in interviews and discussions at public events in towns around the country. One of the fastest-growing festivals is the Literary Festival at Hay-on-Wye, a small town just inside Wales, built on the River Wye on the border with England. It started in 1988 and now, for nearly two weeks each May, about 80,000 booklovers visit this town of less than 2,000 residents, but hundreds of thousands of books.

The books are housed in about 30 second hand bookshops. Some of them are big: one shop used to be the town's old fire station; another one was a cinema. Hay is the biggest literary festival, but its success has inspired others. Another popular one, in the autumn, is held at Cheltenham in central England.

Reading Comprehension

3. A literary festival is held at Hay-on-Wye,
    a. a small town in England with 80,000 visitors who love books.
    b. a Welsh town with 2,000 residents and many more books.
    c. a town on the River Wye with 80,000 resident booklovers.

Part 3   Arts festivals

There are three internationally-famous music and theatre festivals held in various parts of Britain each summer. Probably the best-known, attracting thousands of visitors, is the Edinburgh Festival. It has both an 'official' festival and an 'unofficial' festival called the *Fringe*. Each lasts between three and four weeks. The official festival features classical music, theatre and visual arts, including film; the Fringe mainly features comedy theatre and comedians. Together, they seem to take over

Welcome to Britain

the whole city: the Fringe puts on about 2,000 different shows in more than 250 different venues! It's hard to find a free hotel room in or around the Scottish capital in August because so many festival visitors and performers book them. For a few weeks every summer, Edinburgh becomes a very lively, cosmopolitan city.

In Wales the biggest arts festival is called the Royal National Eisteddfod. It's a competition for poets, choirs, musicians, and dancers and it's held in a different town every year at the beginning of August. It's said to have started in 1176, making it one of the oldest festivals in Europe. About 6,000 competitors take part and about 150,000 visitors attend. The festival also promotes Welsh culture and the Welsh language.

Also in August there are the Promenade[1] music concerts in London. These are a series of concerts designed to make classical music easier for young people, especially, to enjoy. The tickets are cheaper than usual and the seats are taken out of the main hall so the audience can stand, or walk around. These concerts are informally called 'the Proms', and most are also broadcast on BBC television and radio. ■

NOTES
[1] Promenade means to walk, or a place where you can walk.

A poster advertising the Proms concerts and (right) the Royal Albert Hall in London, where the Proms take place.

*R*eading *C*omprehension

4. Which is the best festival to go to if you're interested in comedy?
    a. The Edinburgh Festival.
    b. The Edinburgh Fringe.
    c. The Royal Eisteddfod.

5. At which festival is it possible to walk around during a concert?
    a. The Proms.
    b. The Royal Eisteddfod.
    c. The Edinburgh Festival.

Chapter 15 The arts

In Britain film is considered entertainment more than part of 'the arts' high culture. It doesn't get much government support and lots of British actors, directors and writers work with Hollywood studios. But although Britain makes few films, some are successful internationally and at the Academy Awards. In recent years these have included:

The Kings Speech, Slumdog Millionaire, The Queen, Love Actually, Notting Hill, Bend It Like Beckham, Bridget Jones's Diary, Shakespeare in Love, The Full Monty, Trainspotting, Four Weddings and a Funeral

Structure Practice

a. Choose the one underlined word or phrase that should be corrected or rewritten. Then change it.

1. The longest <u>run</u> theatre production in the world is *The Mousetrap* from the book by Agatha Christie. It <u>opened</u> in London in 1952, <u>passed</u> the record number of performances of 23,074 in 2008 and it's still <u>being performed</u> every night!

2. Hay-on-Wye became a booklover's town because a resident called Richard Booth <u>keep</u> collecting so many books that he <u>had to</u> buy the town's old <u>fire station</u> and then many other cheap <u>properties</u> to house them.

b. Choose the one word or phrase that best completes the sentence.

3. 60% of the population has a library card so they can .... books, CDs and DVDs from their local public library.

   a. borrow   b. lend   c. remove   d. steal

4. The British Library has more than 13 million books, including 6,000 different .... of Shakespeare's plays.

   a. books   b. editions   c. languages   d. performances

5. The venue for the Royal National Eisteddfod .... each year between somewhere in north Wales with a place in south Wales.

   a. alternates   b. alternatives   c. chooses   d. locates

Welcome to Britain

Listening Challenge

Listen and fill in the missing words.

1. Richard Booth, who started the Hay festival, ... in the .... just outside the town, and calls himself the .... of ....

2. To .... for the arts, the government gives some money which it .... buying National Lottery ....

3. Two of the world's oldest auction houses for .... of ...., Sotheby's and Christie's, ... in London in the ....

4. London has several world-famous .... and ....

5. In recent years, several .... have appeared on stage in London because appearing .... at the .... of English-speaking .... increases their credibility as ....

Going Further (for discussion or research)

1. Which of the arts are you interested in?

   ....

2. Name some British artists—actors, directors, painters, sculptors, musicians, or writers (except for Shakespeare and J. K. Rowling):

   ....
   ....

3. Which piece of British work have you seen or read or heard?

   ....

4. Which arts festival (in Britain or Japan) would you most like to go to?

   ....

Chapter 16

Homes, gardens and the countryside

Climbing stiles is normal on a countryside walk. The stiles (fences with steps) are to stop farm animals escaping.

Vocabulary Focus

Match the words in the table with their definition below. Write the word on the line.

afford	suburb
elegant	tool
privacy	wise

tools   1. equipment to do work using your hands

_____ 2. to have enough money to pay for something

_____ 3. a mainly residential area outside the centre of a city or large town

_____ 4. stylish, graceful

_____ 5. a situation which allows you to be private, to do things without other people seeing you

_____ 6. sensible and good (judgements or decisions)

Part 1   Background

'An Englishman's home is his castle' is an old saying. Few Englishmen have ever lived in a castle, but the phrase shows the importance to the English of having their own private living space. And for many people, a house in the country means success. It's notable that lots of suddenly rich working-class and lower middle-class pop stars from towns buy big houses in the country. They move partly for lots of space, partly for privacy, and partly for nature.

Only 1% of Britain's workers are farmers, but the countryside covers almost 70% of the land. Its residents have always been a mix of classes[1]. But increasingly, only well-off people can afford to buy even the small, pretty cottages. And, as shops and schools, and pubs and post offices have closed, many young families have had to move to towns. Many village houses only have residents at weekends as they've been bought by wealthy bankers who work in London.

Most people who live in the centre of London are either rich home owners or not rich at all, renting. The majority of the population lives in the suburbs from where they can get to work and buy a home. About 65% of British people own their home, but it's getting harder for young people to afford one. A house with a garden is ideal. Gardening is one of the most popular leisure activities for about half the population. People feel that having nature nearby improves their quality of life.

Dove Cottage in the Lake District, north w England, was the home of the poet Willian Wordsworth from 1799 to 1808. It gets ab 70,000 visitors a year.

NOTES
[1] But not races. Nearly everyone living in the country is white.

*R*eading *C*omprehension

1. Which statement is true?
   a. Every Englishman's home is like a castle.
   b. No one who is successful wants to live in the countryside.
   c. English people think they should control what happens in their homes.

2. One point which links the centre of London and the countryside is that
   a. a lot of the home owners are rich.
   b. 65% of the British population lives there.
   c. many shops, schools and pubs have closed there.

Hay stacks

Chapter 16 Homes, gardens and the countryside

Part 2 National flowers and public parks

(L) Kew Gardens has a Japanese garden with 灯籠.
(R) Deck chairs on a summer's day in a London park.

Each of the UK's countries has its own national flower. For England, it's the rose; for Scotland, the thistle; for Wales, the daffodil or leek (a vegetable the Welsh grow a lot of); and for Ireland, the shamrock, a kind of plant with three leaves. Across the UK, national parks such as the Lake District, the Peak District and Snowdonia attract millions of British people and foreign tourists. They visit them for walking, picnicking and just driving through.

There are some wonderful private and public gardens all over Britain. One of the biggest and best is Kew Gardens in west London; it includes a Japanese garden. London has more than 11,000 public parks and parks are an important feature of every town. Some new towns built in the last century included the word *garden* in their name to make them sound attractive: examples are Welwyn Garden City and Hampstead Garden Suburb.

There are many different kinds of roses. This one is called Ice Cream.

*R*eading *C*omprehension

3. From the information in the text, what are the *shamrock* and *11,000*?
   a. Scotland's national flower and the number of national parks.
   b. Wales's national flower and the number of London's public parks.
   c. Ireland's national flower and the number of London's public parks.

Part 3 D-I-Y and house words

Suburban houses built early in the 20th century were made to last a long time. Rather than knocking them down and building something new, people prefer to refurbish[3] them, replacing parts and adding others. D-I-Y, which stands for Do-It-Yourself, is one of the most popular leisure time activities. Many people spend their weekends working on their home and going to D-I-Y shops to buy tools and materials for both D-I-Y and gardening. This is especially true when the economy is doing well and people see their home as an investment.

Except in recessions, property often has been a wise financial investment. Both TV and the printed media spend a lot of time and space on the property market. Some inner city houses built in the 18th and 19th centuries are some of the most elegant buildings you will see in Britain, so these often go up in value.

Many words describe the different kinds of homes. We met *cottage* in part 1, paragraph two. In towns people usually live in a *terraced* or a *semi-detached* house. The former is one of a group of houses joined together side-by-side[4]; the latter is a house which is joined to another house on one side, but not joined on the other side. Richer people live in *detached* houses, which are not joined to any other homes. These are more common in the outer suburbs, or the countryside. A *bungalow* (originally an Indian word) means a house on one floor, with no stairs going up or down. Don't let Japanese give you the wrong impression about *mansion*. It's not a *flat*, the British English word, or an *apartment*, the American English word which is becoming increasingly used in Britain. A mansion is an enormous, elegant house which only the very rich can afford. ∎

NOTES
[3] Refurbish is often changed by Japanese English into 'reform'.
[4] In American English it is known as a row house.

*R*eading *C*omprehension

4. The picture on the left is of a
   a. terraced house.   c. bungalow.
   b. semi-detached house.   d. mansion.

5. The picture on the left is of a
   a. terraced house.
   b. semi-detached house.
   c. bungalow.
   d. mansion.

*S*tructure *P*ractice

a. **Choose the one underlined word or phrase that should be corrected or rewritten. Then change it.**

1. If you <u>live on</u> the 1st floor in Britain, or in any European country, you <u>live upstairs</u> because the usual entrance level floor <u>is called</u> the ground floor and the 1st floor is <u>equal the</u> 2nd floor in Japan or America.

2. The <u>high regard</u> English people have for flowers, <u>special</u> the national flower, <u>is shown</u> in the use of <u>the word</u> *rosy* to mean healthy (as in 'rosy cheeks'), and bright, cheerful and good (as in 'the situation looks rosy').

b. **Choose the one word or phrase that best completes the sentence.**

3. An official survey showed that about 80% of .... the households in England are a kind of house, while only 20% are flats, or apartments.

   a. all   b. some   c. many   d. none

4. *Mowing the lawn*, which means cutting the grass in the garden .... called a lawnmower, is one of those household chores[5] someone has to do every few weeks.

   a. in a machine   b. to a machine   c. at a machine   d. with a machine

   NOTES
   [5] chore「雑用」

5. In recent years many pubs have closed, as more people buy their beer and wine more cheaply from supermarkets and drink with friends and family .... home.

   a. in   b. at   c. at the   d. to

Listening Challenge

Listen and fill in the missing words.

1. One fine example of the British .... is the Glover Residence in Glover Garden in ....

2. The house in Glover Garden, which .... for the .... Thomas Glover in .... , is the oldest western style house .... in ....

3. The colour of the national .... is .... with a .... centre.

4. One of the most .... and .... in the English .... is the Chelsea Flower Show in London in ....

5. British people are known as .... - .... / .... are the most popular pets, and .... are slightly more popular ....

Going Further (for discussion or research)

1. What kind of home would you most like to live in?

   ....

2. What are 2 good and 2 bad points of living in the city?

   ....

3. What are 2 good and 2 bad points of living in the countryside?

   ....

   ....

The Cotswold Way passes through Somerset and Gloucestershire in west central England. Popular for hiking, it's 164 kms long.

NATIONAL PARKS

● National Parks Family

● Areas of Outstanding Natural Beauty

Areas of Outstanding Natural Beauty

16	Northumberland Coast	40	Kent Downs
17	Solway Coast	41	Isles of Scilly
18	North Pennines	42	Cornwall
19	Arnside and Silverdale	43	North Devon
20	Forest of Bowland	44	Tamar Valley
21	Nidderdale	45	South Devon
22	Howardian Hills	46	Quantock Hills
23	Anglesey	47	Blackdown Hills
24	Clwydian Range	48	East Devon
25	Lincolnshire Wolds	49	Dorset
26	Lleyn	50	Cranborne Chase and West Wiltshire Downs
27	Shropshire Hills	51	Isle of Wight
28	Cannock Chase	52	Chichester Harbour
29	Norfolk Coast	53	High Weald
30	Gower	54	Sperrins
31	Wye Valley	55	Binevenagh
32	Malvern Hills	56	Causeway Coast
33	Cotswolds	57	Antrim Coast and Glens
34	Chilterns	58	Lagan Valley
35	Dedham Vale	59	Strangford Lough
36	Suffolk Coast and Heaths	60	Lecale Coast
37	Mendip Hills	61	Mourne
38	North Wessex Downs	62	Ring of Gullion
39	Surry Hills		

National Parks Family

1. Cairngorms
2. Loch Lomond and the Trossachs
3. Northumberland
4. Lake District
5. Yorkshire Dales
6. North York Moors
7. Peak District
8. Snowdonia
9. Broads
10. Pembrokeshire Coast
11. Brecon Beacons
12. Exmoor
13. South Downs
14. New Forest
15. Dartmoor

Britain has 15 national parks and 62 official areas of natural beauty. They are not all countryside; most of them also contain roads and small towns.

自習用音声について

本書各章の本文 Part 1, Part 2, Part 3 の音声は以下より無料でダウンロードできます。
予習、復習にご利用ください。

https://www.otowatsurumi.com/3838/

上記 URL をブラウザのアドレスバーに直接入力して下さい。
データサイズの大きなファイルですので、無線 LAN (Wi-Fi) に接続できる環境での利用を推奨致します。
ダウンロードしたファイルは圧縮ファイルですので解凍（展開）してご利用下さい。

Welcome to Britain
[Revised Edition]

英国の〈いま〉を知りたい ［改訂新版］

編著者　Tim Knight
発行者　山口　隆　史

発 行 所　株式会社 音羽書房鶴見書店
〒113-0033　東京都文京区本郷3-26-13
TEL 03-3814-0491
FAX 03-3814-9250
URL: http://www.otowatsurumi.com
e-mail: info@otowatsurumi.com

2018年 3 月 1 日　　初版発行
2025年 4 月 1 日　　9 刷発行

組版　ほんのしろ
装幀　熊谷有紗（オセロ）
印刷・製本　（株）シナノ パブリッシング プレス
■ 落丁・乱丁本はお取り替えいたします。

E-145